THINK LESS! GOLF!

How to play better golf
just by changing th

By Dean Harris

(A book written by an amateur golfer for all golfers)

© THINK LESS! GOLF!

First published in Great Britain by Harris Publishing Ltd in 2024
Oaksey, Wiltshire SN16

A CIP catalogue record for this book is available from the British Library.

ISBN 978-1-8046-7809-1

Printed in Great Britain by BookVault, Peterborough

Dedicated to Clare, Dexter and Felicity,
and all the golf widows/loved ones that allow the golfers in the family to spend hours and days away to play golf, have fun and be social without them.

Cover designed by SJ Taylor Consulting Ltd

www.simontaylorconsulting.co.uk

INDEX

PROLOGUE

This isn't the first book about golf or golf mentality, and it certainly won't be the last, but this will be a great weapon in your armoury when it comes to starting, or adding to, your golf book collection.

My suggestion is to buy/read as many books about golf as possible. They will all provide valuable insights into how to improve your game and scores.

Golf is a sport where you learn as you play, but it is also one of the few sports where you will also get better by reading about it.

Whether starting or continuing your journey to better golf, you won't be disappointed with this book.

Before I get you reading into the main focus of this book, I want to start by telling you what this book is NOT about, to avoid any preconceptions that I'm about to make you a world class player once you've finished reading it or that I'm going to change the physical attributes of how you hit the ball.

If you've purchased this book, then you probably already have a love/hate relationship with the game.

If you don't yet have that love/hate relationship, be prepared for it!

It's most likely you already know how to swing a club and hit a ball, and you have a good grasp on your personal physical ability.

Or maybe you're new to the game of golf, haven't been playing long, but have been out on the course a few times and have hit some balls. Whichever it is, this will either be a refresher or an eye-opening introduction to the psychological side.

'Success in golf depends less on strength of body, more on strength and mind of character.'

Arnold Palmer

PROLOGUE

So firstly, I'm not here to tell you how to physically play golf or how to improve/change your swing mechanics.

If you've been playing for a while, your swing has either become natural or you've had lessons. If you've just taken up playing golf, I recommend getting lessons either during or after you've read this book. You will see from the index that there is a chapter on this topic later on.

Secondly, I'm also not going to give advice on the best shots to take and when. That's all part of your own personal ability and I don't personally know your capabilities or distances. Maybe you don't know them yet yourself if you're just starting out, so that is something to learn from a PGA pro.

What I am going to focus on, in a short, simple, concise and easy to follow manner, is how to categorise your thoughts, and when those thoughts should be used, remembered or forgotten.

I'll introduce you to the 90%/10% timing split and how it impacts the game.

I'll help with ideas of what to think and what not to think about, and when those thoughts help or hinder your play.

I'll also provide templates and pullouts at the end, which you'll come to understand as you read through the book, that can be used when you get out to play and look to improve your game on the course, or gain experience the more you play.

Some of what you read you might already know, but there will also be something you've forgotten or are learning for the first time, that you didn't know about before.

Let me ask a couple of questions to get your mind going for a minute.

1. What is the basic objective of golf?

Take a few seconds to think about an answer to see if it's the same as mine. If not, think about my answer compared to yours and see which makes more sense.

My long answer is: to get the ball in the hole in an area of the green by hitting it in as few shots as possible on multiple sections of a golf course after starting off from a tee (simply put, score as little shots as possible on each hole).

Now, my second question.

2. What is YOUR objective of golf?

Is it to play socially with friends and family? Maybe as part of your business to entertain a customer.

Is it just to get out of the house for a few hours?

Or do you want to play competitively and feel you're playing the best you can but still can't score better?

Would you like to improve but not sure how to or what is stopping you?

Or are you new to the game and don't yet realise how the mind affects golf?

If you're not interested in learning or improving the golf mentality, then this is not the book for you, but if you want to start playing better than your friends and/or family, be able to entertain customers or business partners with a good game of golf, get a lower score than usual when just popping out for a few holes, or want to compete to be in contention instead of just being part of the pack, then you'll relate to a lot, if not all, of what is written in the following chapters.

Finally, a bit about me and why I am writing this book.

At time of writing, I am currently a mid-high handicap golfer and I know it's not related to my swing. I enjoy golf and I can't get enough of it, but my handicap is not improving as quick as I'd like it to. When I get out to play a round, there is always a bad hole or 2 impacting my score. I want to get better and I know it's in my mind, so I started putting pen to paper and considered what I think about when playing golf and what puts me off or distracts me, affecting my rounds.

Since writing my own thoughts, I have put them into practice and my scores have started improving. I became more focused, better prepared and less distracted.

Then I thought that while I help myself, I could also help others.

I took up golf when I was 26, and only played in society days on various different courses around West London and the surrounding counties.

I joined Oaksey Park GC in 2021, the first club I have ever joined, after a 5-year break and I now play competitive and social games regularly.

I have even got my young son playing too.

I am personally ready to improve my own game and I need to change my mentality to do it. I will continue to follow my own advice, and by sharing what I have learnt, I hope other players can improve their mental game and their scores too.

You can see and follow my progress on MyEG (or England Golf). You'll find me under my home course of Oaksey Park GC in Wiltshire.

If I can do it, any golfer can, and I wish I had a book like this when I started playing.

So, without further ado, let's move onto the nitty gritty and look to change the way you think so you can lower your scores.

Enjoy the book and enjoy a better golf mentality.

Dean Harris

1 THE 90%/10% TIMING SPLIT

Golf is a game of numbers and statistics, so let's do a little maths to introduce you to the 90%/10% timing split when out playing a round, and explain what it means to the game.

On average, a four-ball is expected to finish 18 holes of golf in around 4hrs 15mins (or 255mins total).

A mid-high handicapper is expected to hit between 90 and 100 shots, including putts.

If each shot, from the start of the backswing all the way through to hitting the ball and watching it land, takes approximately 15 seconds, you would actually only spend approximately 25 minutes in total hitting the ball. That's inclusive of long putts and short, simple tap ins to finish the holes. 25 minutes of a 4hr 15min round is ~10%.

So, what happens during the other 90% and what goes through your mind in that time?

> 'You swing your best when you have the fewest things to think about.'
>
> Bobby Jones

Let's walk through many of the different scenarios (and I doubt I am even able to consider all of them, so think about other scenarios that you've experienced too).

When you're at the tee box, you're already in a waiting period – either you've taken the first shot and need to wait for the rest of the group to take their tee shots, or they're going first and you're the one waiting to go – whichever it is, what are you thinking? You might be watching their swings and shots to see how they do or if you can learn something from a better player.

You might be focusing on your own swing mechanics and practicing some air shots in preparation for your turn if you're still to go, or you might be talking to the other players while you wait (remember your etiquette when someone takes their swing though).

But when it's your turn to tee off, are you ready? Are you focused? Do you take your time to think about what you've just seen the other players do or, if going first, do you think about the pressure to pull off a good shot? Whatever it is that you're thinking, it's taking time to get ready for your shot.

You follow your pre-shot routine (if you have one, more on this later in the book) and do your setup. Then you swing away, hit the ball and watch it fly off into the distance. What happens next?

You all gather up your bags & trollies, and walk towards your balls for the next shot. This is more time to think and ponder on the shot you've just taken, other players shots, other players scores, your own scores, what you need to do to score well, what you think you should do on the next shot before you've even seen the lie or distance. Maybe you've hit a wayward shot and need to look for your ball, or another player needs help finding theirs – it's always more time to think and less time hitting the ball – more of the 90% and less of the 10%.

Maybe use this time to talk about something other than golf with the other players.

Now, everyone has found their ball and will prepare for the next shot. Again, each player takes their shots in turn, you're back to playing then waiting or waiting then playing. It's more time to consider your options, more time to think about other things before you focus on the shot you're about to take. More of the 90% being taken up.

Your next shot is an approach to the green, but the group in front are still putting out and taking their time, which is taking up your time. You know you can reach so can't risk playing. You stand and wait, you think about your shot or how many you've hit so far, or even how many your opponents have hit so far. You need to focus on the shot at hand, but you're still using up the 90% until you can move on and hit the ball.

Other time-consuming actions before you hit a ball and move into the 10% area are club decision making, target finding and aiming, pre-shot routines, practice swings and setup routines.

Now, you've all made it to the green. You think about the putt you have, or what putts the other players have. You think about how many shots it has taken to get there, or how many putts you must take to make sure of a good score.

You spend time lining up your putt but you're also waiting for others to line their ball up and each take their putts in turn. More time to think, while you are holding the flag or walking the green, getting all your angles and lines sorted.

You finally get to putt and make it to the hole. You get your ball and put the flag back in, or watch someone do it for you. You walk off the green counting your shots, writing your score down, telling the others your score or maybe asking the other players for theirs, before moving off to the next tee and starting the process all over again.

Finally, after 18 holes of this, you've spent approximately 90% doing many other things, or thinking of anything else, instead of hitting the ball, which is the main purpose of the game.

A lot of this time could cause distractions or thoughts that impact your golf and scores.

It is a lot of time to be spent thinking, sometimes more often about bad shots than good ones too, or getting angry that the hole hasn't been played to how you would have liked it to or envisioned it to go, or a good shot ended up in a bad lie.

Anything can happen in golf. No shot is ever the same again. You need to make sure that the 90% playing time where you are not hitting a ball, is kept in focus for when you do take your turn to hit the ball. Keep your time positive and relaxed. Keep the other players positive. No part of the 90% should be spent negatively or dwelling on past bad shots of the round, or if playing the same course again, of past rounds.

Also consider that every golfer is different. Club sets, lengths and styles impact the way people play. Everyone has a different swing and arc. Different makes of ball take different flights once hit, so only focus on how you swing and not your playing partners or opponents.

This is where the following chapters will help. They will provide a mentality to keep your game positive, irrespective of what happens from each shot.

Ultimately this book is intended to improve your scores by utilizing the 90%/10% timing split effectively and positively.

Any thoughts about how you swing should be considered when having lessons, which is also a good time to think about gapping sessions – getting to know your club distances.

Fundamental #1: Planning the Round

I have put this as the first of many fundamentals because, in my opinion, it's the most important.

You'll need a small notebook and pen for this one. Ideally something you can carry in your pocket while playing, as you'll be looking at it regularly throughout the round and mostly before each shot – read on to understand why.

So, what do I mean by planning the round?

A standard golfer will turn up to a golf course and play each hole as they come to it. They might have a hole planner, which outlines the shape and distances of the hole, and play their shots using any club they are confident with or feel is most appropriate at that moment.

I'm not saying this is wrong, for most golfers it works that way, but is it the right mentality to be unprepared for the round ahead?

Let me use an analogy to explain this.

> 'By failing to prepare, you are preparing to fail.'
>
> Benjamin Franklin

When going on a journey, you don't just get in the car and drive somewhere, there will always be a start and a finish.

If you don't know where you're going, you'd use a map or route finder first. These days, put an address into a GPS or SatNav and you'll be led to your destination step by step. Even if you do know where you're going, you'd still like to find the quickest and safest route.

It's the same on a golf course – each hole has a start and a finish, and you need the quickest and safest route.

By planning your round, either the night before or on the morning of your tee time, just like you've planned a route to a destination, you know where you're going and how to get there, and also what to do when you arrive.

For example, let's say you're driving to a golf competition at a new course. You've never played there before so you need to know your route and journey. You also remember you need to stop for fuel on the way, so you'd factor this in too. Finally, you need to know where to park when you arrive. Ideally, you'd park at the first place you stop, but just in case it's full, you will have already considered a backup plan.

Now turn this into a golf hole – leaving the starting point of your journey is the equivalent to your tee shot.

Where it lands will be the equivalent of your fuel stop, with the next shot from that location being the approach shot.

Leaving the fuel stop, the next part of your journey is to your destination – this is the equivalent to being the approach shot to the green, where you'll finish the hole.

This makes the parking part the final step of the journey, and also the final part of each hole, which is your putting. Remember when I said you might not find a parking spot at the first attempt, this could be considered as your first putt.

You go for the hole on your first attempt and one of two things will happen. If it goes in, this is the same as if you found your parking spot straightaway. However, if it misses, you'll have a 2nd chance to make it, and this is the equivalent of your parking spot plan B.

So, another thing to consider when planning your round is wayward shots – what if your tee shot ends up in a different location than planned or the approach shot misses the green? In the journey analogy, this would be thought of as a diversion.

The destination is the same, you just need to find an alternative route back to the plan. In other words, a shot out of the woods back onto the fairway or a chip onto the green.

There are several ways to plan your round – there are golf apps for smartphones which let you view each hole or preview the course hole by hole.

This is not an endorsement but I use, and recommend, Hole19 on my phone for tracking distances, scores and shots (these apps can also be connected to smart watches now, so you don't even have to look at your phone during the round). There are many other good apps, and you should look at basic options before choosing one to subscribe to.

An alternative is to do a web search for the course online and more often than not, depending on the quality of the website and effort the course has put into it, you can get a hole-by-hole overview, maybe some pro tips or download a course planner to see or print.

Another option is to buy a course planner from the pro shop, but this would mean leaving all the hard work to the last minute, and planning each hole as you play it.

Next, when planning your round, you need to factor in club distances, based on clubs you're confident in using or find are really working for you at the moment. For example, if you're struggling to be accurate with the driver off the tee, then use a 3-wood or low iron. Not every hole requires a driver anyway – and this will also become apparent as you plan your round.

Finally, when planning, consider working your way backwards from green to tee. If the app or website uses markers or lines, you can estimate distances from fairways to greens, and tees to fairways.

Using the notebook, make a note of each hole and the distance you'd like your ideal approach to the green to be (don't worry about pin location or putting distances for this, you won't know pin positions until you're approaching each green during play, so it's irrelevant for this).

Here is an example to consider – if your ideal approach shot to the green is from 100-110yds with a pitching wedge, then that's where you want to plan to land your ball from the shot to get you there (for example, a tee shot on a short par 4 or a lay up shot on a par 5).

That's the first plan of action in place – approach to the green by wedge.

The second plan of action will either be the shot you need to make your lay-up distance (for example the 2nd shot on a par 5) or the tee shot on a par 4, to leave you with that 100-110yds approach, as described in the first plan of action. If the lay up only needs to go roughly 150yds, and this is the distance for a 7-iron (as long as your previous shot has landed on or close to where you planned for it, or you only need to hit this distance off the tee), then this would be your planned shot in this instance.

This gives you less to think about when waiting to play your shot or standing over your ball ready to hit.

If hitting a tee shot to get to a safe place and not taking any risks requires a 3-wood instead of a driver, and this covers 210-220yds to leave a 9-iron for 120-130yd approach, then you'll know that's the best club to use.

Also, when planning your round, you will discover where the hazards are that need to be avoided, so you can see them and plan to target away from them ahead of time.

Longer tee shots obviously require the driver, but like I said, most holes don't need a driver if it's a riskier or less confident shot.

Finally, on some holes, there will be a 3rd plan of action, and this would be the tee shots of par 5's (tee shot – lay-up – approach would be the 3 plans here).

This plan of action is to get you into your preferred position for the lay-up shot, if it's not an option to reach the green in two.

If at any point your shot doesn't work out as planned, think of the diversion analogy – all you need to do is figure out the best and safest way to get back on the original route without taking any unnecessary risks, and still giving you the best chance of keeping the score down.

Don't overthink it.

There will also need to be contingencies in your planning, as things change during the round. Be open to adapting the shot and club selections. The weather can play a part in requiring to club up or down (wet or windy conditions), bad bounces into an undulating landing area or rough, off target hitting or landing in bunkers. Even hills that you can't see in 2D pictures that are a part of the course when you get there require a different thought process. Planning gives you a headstart. It will not always be accurate on the day, but it will provide you with a better idea of what lies ahead, leaving less guess work and more stability in your club selection making.

By planning ahead, not only does it give you an insight into the course you're about to play, it gives you preparation ahead of time and should reduce the chance to overthink your shots on the day.

It will help to limit the chance of risk by choosing clubs confidently and considering distances in advance (more on this in later chapters).

It will also give you an edge over your competitors/playing partners when it comes to less thinking and, ideally, less hitting too.

You'll always have that 90%/10% timing split during your round, but wouldn't you rather know you can relax between shots than worry about what to do next or what happened before?

Something to take away from this chapter:

Plan the action so you action the plan!

Fundamental #2: Only Focus on the Current Shot

I know it seems like I'm stating the obvious in this chapter by saying to focus on the current shot for a game where each shot is played one at a time, but mentally it's a lot more difficult than you realise, especially after a few bad shots or a bad round, and maybe you've never noticed before how much thought is not about the current shot as you apply your pre-shot routine and setup, or as you're about to hit the ball.

The reason for this chapter is to help you realise and stop any errant thoughts as you're about to hit each ball, because it's important to shut everything out except what you want to do with your swing and shot – even then, there shouldn't be anything to think about, you should be able to 'switch off' from pre-shot routine, through setup, through your backswing and downswing and through hitting the ball, not 'switching back on' until you've finished watching your ball land and settle.

For every shot over 9 or 18 holes, or however many you are playing when you go out on the course, there shouldn't be any distractions impacting your next shot, whether it be off the tee, from the fairway, recovering from the rough or anywhere else on the hole.

> 'The most important shot in golf is the next one.'
>
> Ben Hogan

If anything does distract you, start again with your pre-shot routine and setup, and don't take the shot until you're ready and have 'switched off' or 'in the zone'.

For example, it's very daunting when playing off the first tee with an audience. Maybe the first tee is near the clubhouse and there is a gallery of players who have finished or yet to start their rounds who could be watching, or you're in a competition where everyone is off the first tee in stages.

Whatever the circumstances, there will be at least one other player or spectator watching you and when you realise this, or subconsciously feel it, it often brings negative thoughts: 'what if I duff it or top it and it doesn't go very far?', 'what if I look rubbish?' or 'I don't like people watching in case I have a bad shot'.

When it's out of your control, there's nothing you can do, so you need to overcome this. What you should be thinking before you step onto the tee box must always be positive. You should be stepping up with confidence and your focus should only be on that tee shot. YOUR shot. THIS shot.

If you're anywhere else on the course, then the same applies. Forget your surroundings, only focus on the current shot – hence the importance of this chapter.

As long as you only focus on your pre-shot routine, your target (something I talk about in a later chapter), your setup and hit the ball confidently and like you're playing on your own, only one thing will happen and you'll hit a great shot. Also remember you've already thought out what you are going to do if you have planned your round, so you're already off to a good start if your shot has gone where you wanted it to, and your focus on the current shot has put you in the ideal position for the next one.

So the next time you're playing in a large competition or society day with multiple tee times and a big group of players gathered on the first tee, or you're out on the fairway and other players watch while you take your shot, forget the overwhelming feeling and pressure to hit a great shot, you now have your own way of dealing with it and you have learnt to 'switch off' so that you can be positive and confident in your own ability to pull the shot off that only you want and planned for.

If it is a great shot, savour the moment. Record it in a memory bank somewhere, or note it down when you get a chance, and then forget about it for this round. Switch back on while you watch the rest of your group tee off/take their shots and then walk to your next shot head held high.

Any shot you've just taken is in the past for this round. It should not be remembered until the end of the round, or the next time you play the course again. Even then it should just be a short recall of it.

The focus then becomes the next current shot. The here and now. Not the previous shot or what your next shot looks like if all goes to plan – this shot is your new focus. Don't focus on the green yet, and especially don't focus on what you want/need to score, however the hole is going.

Focusing on the current shot is not just about forgetting the previous shot but also not thinking about the future result of this shot or the hole you're playing. It should be OK to walk and talk as you go to your ball, but once there, consider looking at the next part of your plan and see what you need to do to close that plan out for this hole, by playing the current shot. Adapt it if needed to, but only adapt what is needed for this shot to work.

Also, if the plan hasn't worked for the previous shot and you're not in the intended landing zone, don't think about why, but either focus on the recovery, if needed, or continue as if you had stuck with the plan and make a new plan for this hole. Work out how best to close out the hole safely and still with as few shots as possible.

The same goes for putting. Focus on your line, your speed and your touch at this point – forget how you got to the green, you've made it and you don't need to remember now for the time being (you can make notes once you've finished the hole). Don't focus on your score until you've finished the hole either. Take as few putts as possible, the hole on the green you're playing is the only focus and your current shot. Learn all you can about your shot. If you are in a better position than other players on the green, let them putt out first and see what they do, how they swing their putters, how much effort they put in and, if applicable, how much their putt is similar to yours and try to read any impact they had on the same line – this can give a lot away for when you're up to take yours.

Then switch off into focus mode, follow your pre-shot routine (you should have one for putting as well), set your target, setup, swing away and move on. You will always putt well if you have done all you can to get it in the hole on the first attempt.

So far this chapter I have only talked about great shots and positive outcomes, but what happens after a bad shot? The answer is nothing different. Bad shots happen to everyone. The mentality is how you deal with it. Don't get angry, don't dwell on what happened (make a note for later and see if it's something that needs work when on the range or practice areas).

In that moment, just shrug your shoulders and walk away. The shot is done, you can't change it, so move on and get back to positivity. If the shot needs to be taken again (the ball has gone out of bounds or might be hard to find, so you take a provisional), get back to being positive, keep the same routines and play your second ball like you had planned for the first.

There is a saying for this: 'always play your second ball first' – it's as if to say the 2nd shot is always most likely to be how it should have been played first time. If needed, imagine that you've already hit a ball and the one you're now focusing on is the back up. You'll be ready, confident, switched off and play it like you know you can.

If no second ball is needed, then walk onto the next shot and refocus. It's a new shot and a chance to get back to plan. Forget about the past shot, don't think about the future of the hole or the score already, just do your best to find the safest way back to your plan.

Bad shots are definitely frustrating, but you'll find you have more good ones than bad ones in any round. We play golf to enjoy it. We know we can play well, so get back to playing well.

Recovery from bad shots takes patience, so keep in mind it will take some time to get to a stage where bad shots don't matter. It won't always happen immediately.

Bad shots will happen to other players too, so watch and observe their behaviour. In a match or competition, if they get angry after a bad shot, see what they do. You can walk away after a bad shot knowing you will recover. Their reaction might not be a good one, so you can think to yourself 'I'm glad that's not me'.

Anger and negativity only lead to more bad shots, more anger and more negativity. Once in a bad shot cycle, it's hard to break out of it.

The thought process changes to bad targeting, bad routines and setup, or not even bothering anymore.

By being able to walk away from the negatives of golf, being patient and moving on, not only does it make you look like a better person, it will make you a better golfer. You'll have a playing advantage over someone who can't walk away from their bad shots or bad behaviour, and you'll also have other players who will want to play with you again – but they won't be wanting to play golf with a player who can't handle themselves and react badly when something goes wrong.

So, whatever happens from tee to green, remember to stay positive, stick to your plan as much as possible, make sure you 'switch off' and only focus on the current shot each time.

Fundamental #3: Aiming at a Target

You have an action plan and you know how to only focus on each shot being played, now you need to add aiming at a specific target to the list of important fundamentals. This replaces the 'hit in a general direction and hope it lands where I want it to' mindset.

When on the tee box, you go through your pre-shot routine and setup. You're ready to hit the shot, and have a wide, open fairway in front of you, but what are you actually aiming at? Are you just hitting to hope it lands in the middle of the fairway trusting in your swing or do you include targeting as part of your pre-shot routine?

The golfing mind needs a specific target to have the most success at getting the ball to its intended location.

Imagine you're playing catch with someone, you don't just aim in a general direction, you aim specifically at your throwing partner.

You judge the distance for the throw and then focus your mind directly towards the person catching before going through the motions and letting go. Notice how this all comes naturally. It's the same for golf – picking a target in the distance, ideally something small and specific on the line of your intended location, gives your mind a focus so that when you go through your swing motions you will naturally downswing in that direction and, when hitting the ball, it will take off towards the intended target and land in the intended area, or close to it.

A little tip that I use when teeing up my ball is to use a line or mark on the ball (ideally a straight line) to aim towards the distant target upon putting it on the tee. Pick out your distant target and using the ball mark or line, aim it in the same line before you start your pre-shot routine and setup.

'The odds of hitting your target go up dramatically when you aim at it.'

Mal Pancoast

Once you're ready to take the shot, line your club up with the line on the ball (naturally aiming the club towards your target now) and swing away.

If needed, it also helps to take one quick final glance at the distant target before looking back at the ball and starting your backswing. Try not to prolong looking at the distant target and overthink it, you just need to see it quickly for your mindset to envision and acknowledge that direction.

Next come the lay-up and/or approach shots. The principle is the same – aim for a distant target as part of your pre-shot routine and prior to setup.

Unless the course is under winter rules (when pick and place rules apply), you won't be able to use the same tip as the tee shot to line up the ball mark (or line) with the target, so it's all about the line of the downswing.

My tip for this is to estimate and calculate the distance and choose the club you'll be using for the shot. Refer to your hole-by-hole action plan (if you planned your round) and have landed at or near your intended spot from the previous shot. You might need to factor in any contingencies here (weather conditions, current lie or hazards).

Using the club head or shaft, lift it up to get a line of sight to a distant target, then use it to create an imaginary line between the distant target and your ball. Take a mental note of something close to the ball that is on the same imaginary line (a clump of grass or discolouration in the ground, for example) and now you've got distant target and local target markers to use. This will help you align your clubface in the direction of the distant target for when you are ready to setup.

Other things to consider before taking your lay-up or approach shots – if laying up, make sure your distant target is avoiding any hazards and leaves you with an ideal approach distance (refer to action plan, if you have one) or if approaching the green, first think about the distance: anything within 120yds should be targeted at the flag or flagpole (more about the short game and shorter clubs in a later chapter), but if the approach is longer, then you'd still look for a distant target beyond the green (in line with your approach onto the green).

Again, remember to factor in any contingencies (including greenside hazards this time).

Go through your pre-shot routine, apply your setup using the local target mark then check your distant target one more time before looking back at the ball and taking your shot.

Ideally your approach shot has made it onto the green, but if your shot was wayward or took a bad bounce and has left your next shot to be taken from the side of the green, then you'll be lining up for either a chip or a putt (a mental thought to always consider here is to use the putter from off the green where possible. An errant putt is always going to provide a better outcome than an errant chip shot).

From here, you'd check for the best place to land a chip or best line for a putt with the only target being the hole itself. The flagpole is the ideal target, not just because it's in the hole, but also because it's a small, tighter target to aim for that if the ball goes close, it's most likely to end up in the hole, or very close to it.

The contours or slope of the green will always be a factor too, so consider them in your target setting and aiming.

Finally, and most importantly, once you've made it onto the green, your only shot left is the putt, where the only remaining target is the hole and only the hole. No other thought should be in your mind than to reach the hole. Again, I know I'm stating the obvious, but it's a big misconception of putting 'just to get it close'. This doesn't save shots, it adds them.

So, on the green, your accuracy is critical, therefore your aim is to be something small that can be seen from the location of the ball. For straight and flat putts, this could be something like a blade of grass or bit of mud at the back of the hole (I use the farthest part of the top of the white cup inserted into the hole because if the ball hits this, it's in the hole).

Take your time to understand your line, from the front and also behind the hole, to see if there are any turns or undulations along the way. You'd factor these turns in and aim at something that brings the turn into play (often using the hole as a guide, you could think about how many holes to the left or right should the ball be hit, and look for a mark to aim at, that once reached, will impact the roll of the ball as it gets closer to the hole).

Then you just need to bring into play the touch and speed needed to reach that area so that the ball makes its way towards the hole from that new target point.

There is a chapter on putting later on in this book, and I detail the ideal mindset to have, but most importantly remember to make sure you get the ball to the hole, or at least slightly past it if it doesn't go down at the first attempt.

Note: you're not aiming the putt to go close – the objective of golf is the get the ball in the hole in as fewer shots as possible – so go for it! Give it the best chance you can of getting it in the hole with as few putts as possible!

Next chapter is about the importance and mentality of the pre-shot routine.

Fundamental #4: The Importance of a Pre-Shot Routine

Golf is a game of inconsistency. You never hit the same shot consecutively. You never land in the exact same spot twice and, ideally, you'd not be swinging with the same club twice in a row.

> 'A routine is not a routine if you have to think about it.'
>
> Davis Love Jr

On a par 3, you'd ideally use an iron then a putter. If you miss the green from the tee, then the approach club is likely to change and not be the same as the tee shot club.

On a par 4, you'd be hitting a driver or a wood, maybe even a driving iron, if that's a more comfortable and appropriate club for the tee shot. Next, you'd use a mid to short iron for the approach into the green (or lay up then approach if needed), finally followed by the putter (unless chipped or pitched in already).

For a par 5, it's very similar to the par 4, except a lay up is most likely to be essential.

Each hole is inconsistent, they change 18 times in a round (if playing the full course). No hole is exactly the same, and as per the previous chapter, each shot has a different target on each hole.

So, there is only ONE thing that can be consistent on each hole, for each shot, to keep the mindset focused and to hit the ball the way you want each time – that's the pre-shot routine. Your personal preparation for each time you set a target, take practice swings, and apply setup.

When playing off a tee or anywhere from the course, it should be the same. The only time it changes is when you're on the green, as you'd also have a putting pre-shot routine too.

The pre-shot routine consistency will be there to help you switch off and get your mental focus prepared to get the ball to your intended target location.

It's also the one method of your game that brings you back to the present, the current shot. It's the starting point to forgetting any previous shots, putts or holes already played. It should also stop you thinking too far ahead – the only forward-looking process of the pre-shot routine is to identify a target, then you come back to focus on the current shot only.

I cannot tell you what your pre-shot routine should be, as it's very personal to your own preferences and abilities, but it could include practice swings, target setting and aiming, getting your grip ready and, what I feel to be most important, switching off from everything in your surroundings (other players, weather conditions, noises and distractions) and only focusing on the ball.

You should already know which club you will be prepared to use – refer to the action plan if applicable from the current location. You should already have picked out your distant target, mentally noted a local target, and visualized the intended landing location. This just leaves you to follow your consistent routine before setting up and hitting the ball.

The impact of not having a pre-shot routine is going to be errant shots or putts. If you haven't had a practice swing, you rely solely on the trust you'll get it right first time.

A practice swing will help you get comfort and confidence that you will pull the shot off, that your swing is consistent and you'll commit to the shot like you did with the practice swing.

If you haven't found a target, how can you be sure the direction is correct?

Hitting in a general direction could give you a good landing spot, if hit correctly, but could leave you with a bad approach to the green if you haven't considered a smaller intended location with a better approach.

These circumstances could impact the outcome of other shots on the hole, which in turn will impact the score of the hole and the round overall. Remember we're trying to reduce shots per hole, not add to them.

I recommend using your pre-shot routine whenever swinging a club – on the course, down the driving range, in your garden (be aware of your surroundings) or any open land (where ball games are allowed).

When on the course, always consider the inconsistency between clubs, with every club creating a different outcome and not using the same club subsequently, so even when practicing, be inconsistent with your club selection but always consistent with your pre-shot routine.

On the range, change up each club for each shot and practice your pre-shot routine each time – pre-shot routine, hit a driver. Consider what could come next, choose a 7-iron for example, follow your pre-shot routine and then swing away. This could be your practice for a long par 4. Start again with the driver, or maybe a 3-wood this time, but take another tee shot, following your pre-shot routine again. Then consider a lay up shot followed by an approach shot – each time, following your pre-shot routine. This could be sampling a par 5.

If taking irons off the deck or off a tee, these would sample a par 3, but you would always be consistent with your pre-shot routine to get your mentality and confidence prepared for when you're on the course and follow the same methodology.

If you can, practice hitting out of bunkers and apply a pre-shot routine here too. You can't touch the sand with the club head, so any practice swings would be done out of the bunker, but you'd apply everything else the same to the shot each time (stance, setup, dig your feet in and open the club face if practicing for greenside bunkers – more on bunker shots later in the book).

Also, practice putting. Find some drills that could help and keep the mentality the same for each putt, as if you were playing a round – putting is what ultimately brings the scores down, so you'd want to trust everything you do to get it in the hole first time as much as possible.

Note: practice as you play and play as you practice, as long as the pre-shot routine is used and kept consistent.

FUNDAMENTAL #5: AVOIDING HAZARDS AND HAZARD RECOVERY

It's the most daunting and fear-invoking effect in golf – facing a hazard in your line-of-sight to target, but there is a way to get over the fear – keep calm, carry on and mentally overlook it as if it's not even there.

Old habits die hard, but they need to be completely eradicated from your mindset when trying to avoid a hazard in play.

If playing off the tee and there is a hazard in front or nearby, it's very easy to think about it, and thinking about it puts it into your mentality and invokes the obvious fear of hitting the ball into it – and once it's in your mind, there is more chance you will hit into it than there is of missing it. It's a natural reaction to make something worse when you're overthinking trying to avoid something completely.

So, you have to not think about it. Imagine it's not there at all.

> 'Of all the hazards, fear is the worst.'
>
> Sam Snead

I know it's easier said than done, but as long as you follow your pre-shot routine and setup process, and you are ready to hit any shot that's typical when there isn't a hazard in front of you, you're more likely to avoid hitting into it. A normal, accurate, prepared-for shot will fly right over it.

A common thought process when faced with a hazard, especially a water one where you might lose the ball completely, is to use an old ball, one you're not afraid of losing. This mindset alone is a bad one, as it's already considering defeat to the hazard, and means the hazard is in mind and focus. The solution would be to use a ball you would normally hit off the tee (a favourite brand or colour), this will provide confidence that it'll go where you want it to and, as long as you've done your best to make it over the hazard with routines, targeting and setup, you will put trust in yourself to produce the best outcome.

If you're about to play an approach shot into the green, and it's 50% or 75% surrounded by hazards (sand or water), your aim should be to the least surrounded areas, the remaining 25% or 50%. Also consider that if the free-from-hazards and safest area is at the back of the green, give it the best chance of staying safe by aiming for the middle of the green instead of the flag or hole. This way, it will either stay on the green for a putt, or worst-case roll onto the safe area behind and avoid all hazards.

If the distance to the intended location is too risky (or too long on a par 5 maybe), then laying up for a simple wedge or chip over, or around, the hazard would be the safest option. Know your swing and distances, and be confident and committed.

If you happen to have brought a greenside hazard into play, for example missed the green the wrong side of the hazard, then it's a similar mindset to playing off earlier shots where the hazard is in view and therefore in mind – you just have to imagine it's not there when you take your shot. You'd choose your club and shot wisely, but you'd still play the same shot you would play to get close to the hole as if you're aiming for a specific landing point for it to bounce or roll on.

You'd maybe go for a bit more loft to make sure of the height to carry the hazard, but you'd still play the shot with the hazard out of mind and focus.

Be confident, committed and don't overthink it. You've landed in the current position because either you wanted/needed to (ie. laying up) or the previous shot didn't go as intended, but you can't change it so forget about it and make the next shot count like you know you can. Be positive.

I know I am often stating the obvious, or repeating what I have already put in previous chapters, but repetition is the key to remembrance and I am trying to reiterate the objective for safer and fewer shots per hole.

Moving onto getting out of hazards, or recovering from a dropped shot, can also be a daunting prospect, making the risk of finishing the hole with a high score even greater.

It's important not to get downhearted or angry. Hitting into hazards is not always down to a bad shot – maybe you've hit a great shot but got caught out by a bad bounce that deflected into a hazard, or the ground is hard and dry so the ball carried on further than expected and finished in a hazard. Remember how golf is unpredictable and inconsistent.

If you know how to recover from hazards, then you'll know the right shot to play out, but if not, get some lessons from a pro on hazard recovery and practice bunker shots whenever possible.

Fairway bunkers are similar to shots from the rough. You'll not have a great lie, but you should have the opportunity to make a clean shot out, and only require a middle or short iron to still get out with some distance. If you just need to hit it out, a simple short and safe shot would suffice – get back onto your planned route – otherwise, have confidence to swing away like you're hitting an approach shot from the rough.

If you have landed in a greenside bunker, you'll need a bit more skill and finesse to go with your focus and confidence. Also, more commitment than usual comes into play here.

You're not looking to hit it hard or far, so focus on hitting behind the ball and following through with the club head is what your mentality should be. Follow a pre-shot routine before heading into the bunker, and learn how to get your stance correct and have your club face open more than usual for short bunker shots.

If you've hit into a water hazard, you have options for your next shot, allowing for a good recovery and still finish on a decent score despite the dropped shot.

Water hazards either have a specified drop zone or the ball can be dropped anywhere before the hazard but in the line from point of entry. Placed correctly and you can get a good advantage for the approach shot into the green, or laying up if needed. Forget the previous shot once the ball has been placed and get back into the focus of the current shot, as usual.

If you are fortunate enough to land in a dry water hazard, consider the playable option. It's treated like a bunker where you can't touch the ground with your club head before striking the ball, but if there is a clear opportunity to get it out first time without risking a drop shot, and it's a safe outcome, be confident and take it – however, don't risk it unnecessarily – the safer and better option might still be the drop shot and easier approach.

Hazards are a frustrating aspect of golf but also an important part of the challenge. If all holes were just green fairways and open, flat greens, where would the fun be in that? Enjoy the challenge of a hazard, don't think of it as a downside to the round. Be confident, be committed, trust your ability to recover and embrace the chance to make a good shot from an unlucky situation.

Fundamental #6: Commitment, Confidence and Trust

I've already mentioned about being committed and having confidence in previous chapters. Along with trust, they are much needed attributes, not just when facing hazards, but through all aspects of every other shot too.

> 'Courage is going from failure to failure without losing enthusiasm.'
>
> **Winston Churchill**

Each attribute goes hand in hand with the other two –

Confidence comes from being committed to the shot and trusting your swing to pull off a good shot each time.

Commitment is made by trusting your abilities and being confident in your focus to follow your swing and produce the desired outcome.

Trust is built by being confident in your personal golfing ability and commitment to personal improvement.

As well as working hand in hand, they also work on their own.

Let's start with commitment.

There are 2 types of commitment in golf – firstly, the commitment to each shot, following routines, focusing the mind and producing the intended result each time (this comes from playing or practicing regularly). The other is the commitment to yourself – for personal improvement, for achieving results and getting out of the game what you put in.

You can push yourself to learn, either from this book, from lessons with a golf pro or general play on the course, and commit to improve your scores by setting goals (more on this in a later chapter). Life has its obstacles, but when you get any opportunity, commit time to play or practice, and use it to help improve your game.

If you can't leave the house, find time to practice swinging a club in the garden or a local safe space.

If you can get down the range, commit to focus on weaknesses or follow the alternate shot process, to practice as if you were on the course. As per the last chapter, use the mentality of practice to consider what you would do on the course.

Once you've gained experience, or used the practice time, to improve your commitment to yourself and every shot, you will build on your confidence and trust.

Moving onto trust, this is also a two-fold attribute. Firstly, there is the trust in your own personal capability to produce good golf. Do you trust that you've done all you can to perform to your potential every time you play and can you trust yourself to push your potential further?

The second attribute of trust is in your swing. Are you capable of switching off from your surroundings so that you can rely solely on your body and swing mechanics once you're ready to take your shot?

That is the ultimate trust in yourself – you've started the backswing, everything is in motion, trust is letting your natural ability to flow through your downswing and hit the ball exactly as you want to and get it to the intended location during your pre-shot routine.

Trust builds more from confidence gained and commitment given to each shot. You must also have trust in your clubs. A set of clubs is as personal as your underwear. They need to fit your style of play and be comfortable when being used.

When using other clubs – maybe a rental set at another club or while on holiday – they are very generic and will not have a personal feel. It's very hard to get used to them at first, so you have to put a different kind of trust into them. So, when it comes to having your own clubs, you need to make sure they feel right for you or you need to work on getting a set that feels right and you can trust.

They will also help with your commitment and confidence.

Finally, confidence. Golf is a time-consuming sport. It takes a time commitment, something us amateur golfers don't always have. As mentioned earlier, life has obstacles – family, work or other responsibilities – so we have to build confidence, and improve ability, with a limited amount of time.

We take every opportunity to play or practice, and when we do, we need to make sure we are 100% focused for the round or practice session.

We build confidence by doing, by being repetitive, so it's important to have confidence every time we play or practice and we are only likely to gain more of it with every good shot and positive outcome.

All the good shots we have, the more positivity it breeds and the more confident we get – then, when we do get time to play, we can bring that confidence with us. It's also important to keep that confident mindset off the course or practice range too. If you're not playing but think about golf, it's imperative to think positive about it, and keep confident thoughts in your mind (remember the good shots from recent rounds or some of the best holes you've ever played. Refer to your notes if you have any). The next time you play, you will naturally have that confident mentality from the first tee onwards, or when on the range or practice areas. Keep the positivity to continue keeping the confidence.

Positive commitment to your shots when you play and positive trust in your swing will help your confidence grow.

Add these 3 essential building blocks to your growing list of fundamentals to produce great golf and consistently play with a positive and focused mindset.

The next chapter will be about 2 more building blocks in the process to improve your golf and lower your scores – using memories of good shots and forgetting memories of bad shots to keep positive and be resilient.

Fundamental #7: Good Shot Memory over Bad Shot Memory – Positivity and Resilience

If golf is such an inconsistent and frustrating sport, why do we continue to play? A mid-high handicapper, or a beginner, will hit one or 2 good shots before making a typical mistake or errant shot that changes the score on the hole. Or even start the hole with a bad tee shot but recover and close the hole out really well.

It's the good shots that keep us interested. It's the great feeling of an intended shot coming off that keeps us coming back for more. It's the thrive for improvement that keeps us trying to get better. It's also the bad shots that push for correction, or a bad round that had some good shots included which give us confidence that we know we can do better.

Why is golf so addictive when it is so frustrating? Why, after 9 or 18 holes, do we feel the need, and/or want, to continue playing?

If you have a good round and finish with a good score, you want to carry on playing good golf. You feel everything has finally come together that you don't want to lose the great feeling of positivity, or maybe some luck is finally on your side. Even after a bad round, the positivity and resilience from the good shots or good scoring holes, make you feel the need to continue playing because you know there is potential to score better if all those good shots come together in the same round.

So, we strive for good and positive golf over the negativity of a bad shot or score and we keep being resilient over a bad shot or score.

Positivity breeds positivity. It gives us confidence and happiness from our golf. If you focus on the current shot, and the last shot was a good one, you'll most likely have another good shot.

'Do your best one shot at a time and then move on. Remember that golf is just a game.'

Nancy Lopez

Be positive and only remember good shots. If bad thoughts, or bad memories, creep into your mind as you step up to the ball, be resilient and change the focus back to a positive mindset – remember a good shot, either from a previous hole or round. Follow a plan, follow your pre-shot routine, block everything out by switching off, focus on the current shot and as long as you do all you can to produce the shot you want, you will either get the best shot out of it or a very unlucky outcome that you can't do anything about even after doing everything right. There is always luck in golf, sometimes it's not always good.

Our minds naturally have a way of going to the negative over the positive. We always think the worst of things or situations. It's the human mindset to protect the brain from something bad happening, either for the first time or, if it has happened previously, from occurring again, so we can be prepared for the worst and we aren't disappointed when we think it's going to happen anyway.

So, when we step up to the shot, and our mind remembers something negative as we step up to the ball to take a shot, we are overcome with thoughts of it all going wrong rather than the positive of it going exactly right.

Here is an example of a thought process from a possible scenario during a round, as this goes through your mind: 'There is a ditch or water hazard in reach or in front of me, I'll lose a ball and drop a shot if I hit into it', when instead what you should be thinking is 'there's my target, that's where I'm going to hit the ball to when I setup and swing away, so I can hit the intended location for my next shot' – there isn't any thought or mention of a ditch or water hazard because you'd want to avoid any focus on it, not even acknowledge it's there.

As long as you realise that you have a negative thought, you can still change it before you start your pre-shot routine and setup.

When you change it to a positive thought, the shot goes well and you're buzzing.

You're feeling positive and good about yourself. Keep that memory and emotion going, make a note of it for another time, because that will make sure the next shot (or future shots if reading your notes when in a similar situation) follows the same positive feeling.

If a negative thought does pop up and you do have a bad shot, be resilient, shake it off and recover well on the next shot to get the positivity back.

Positivity and resilience are much needed aspects of golf. Commitment, confidence and trust need positivity to grow, but also bring more positivity every time something positive happens.

Resilience from bad shots or bad memories will also help you improve. Focus on the positive, be resilient to the negative, forget the bad moments and cherish the good ones.

Next chapter, I focus on the distractions caused by the surroundings of golf, eliminating fear from the mind, embracing the nerves when feeling under pressure and how to relieve that pressure so it can be avoided.

Fundamental #8: Avoiding Distractions, Eliminating Fear, Embracing Nerves & Relieving Pressure

Golf is one of the very few sports, if not the only one, where you spend more time not playing than you are playing.

> 'If you believe it'll work out, you'll see opportunities. If you don't believe it'll work out, you'll see obstacles.'
>
> Wayne Dyer

During the non-playing time, the previous chapters should help change your mindset and preparations, but when it comes to playing your shots, it's like a rollercoaster ride at a large theme park – you wait ages to take the shot, follow your pre-shot routine and setup and then, once you've hit the ball, it's all over until the next shot when you do it all again. When not playing your shot, it's easy to relax and talk to other players, take in the scenery or enjoy watching other golfers. This can cause a delay in your momentum. As so much goes on while you wait, it's very typical that when you're about to take your shot something will go through your mind to impact how you hit the ball. It could be something you see or hear, or it could be a thought from a bad memory, you could be overthinking your current shot or just not focused at all.

Your shots will only improve and be good if you are in a 'bubble' of focus, where nothing can distract you between setting up and the ball landing.

It's easier to read this than it could be to put into practice, so you'll need to come up with a way to focus yourself for each shot that allows you to do this.

Maybe close your eyes for a few seconds and take deep breaths before starting your setup and taking your shot. A relaxed shot is better than a distracted one.

Don't think about your total score until the end of the round. Worrying about the score on each hole or as you go round is more likely to impact it than improve it.

If you think about scoring, not only is it distracting, but it will also add pressure to the shot you're about to play. You could be considering what you need to score to finish the hole better than a previous round or against another player, so you then put pressure on the shot because of the need to get it close to the intended target to finish the hole well, where it would be better to just relax and take the shot no matter the outcome of the hole at this point. Thinking about your score on each hole or round as you play rather than as you finish (either each hole or round), means you're not focusing on the current shot – you're thinking about the past and the future (what you've hit so far and what you want to hit to finish with a good score).

Change this mindset and you can relieve some of the pressure this adds to an already frustrating game.

Eliminating physical, visual and thought distractions is one thing to practice, on and off the course, but there are other distractions in our emotions – fear, nerves and pressure.

How do we eliminate those to be able to relax and focus on our golf?

Let's start with fear – what do you fear? Once you answer that, you can work to eliminate it. Is it fear of embarrassment if a shot is hit terribly? Or is it a fear of letting a partner or team down in a matchplay round or during a competition?

Fear itself is possible to overcome if you control it from the mind and not let it get to you.

Everybody fears hitting it badly, but if you switch the fear to relaxation, follow your target setting, pre-shot routine and setup, the fear should eliminate itself because you know you have done all you can, physically and mentally, to perform the shot you want.

Revert to my previous chapter on confidence, commitment and trust – these aspects also help eliminate fear.

Good shot memories, as explained in chapter 8, will also help reduce or eliminate fear.

Get into an 'I can do this' mindset, be positive and the fear will disappear.

Let's move onto pressure, how it could impact play and be reduced or relieved.

Golf should be a calm, relaxed game. There shouldn't be any pressure, but it still happens, either naturally or deliberately, and this can affect your shots.

Firstly, you need to overcome personal pressure. This can be caused by your own high expectations. Whatever your level, beginner or experienced, you can only play to a certain standard until you improve.

Don't feel that you have to play better golf shots or score better on each hole, if that's not your current level of play. As you improve, those shots and results will come naturally.

Trying to hit shots you're not yet capable of, or are good enough to do but are out of form or practice, will only increase the pressure you feel and will make you produce bad shots.

Relieve the pressure on yourself by doing everything you usually do to produce the intended shot. No matter what happens, you can say you did all you could to hit the ball the way you wanted to and focused on the best outcome, putting no pressure on yourself and played the shot relaxed.

Secondly, there will always be an element of peer pressure, either from a playing partner or team that is relying on you to produce a shot they need in a competition, or from an opponent who wants you to do badly to give them a better chance of winning.

A good partner or team will encourage or motivate, they shouldn't need to apply pressure or leave you to be the only one to make the best shot, and you shouldn't feel it if you have confidence that you can do what they need you to do, if they've failed to get the best outcome from their shots. You'll pull off the best shot possible if you ignore the pressure of the moment and play your own game for that shot. You can then walk away with pride knowing that you've done something to help your partner or team on that hole, once you've had the intended outcome. They'll be pleased too, and will know that a relaxed shot was better than a pressurized one.

If you're being put under pressure by an opponent during a matchplay round, whether it be from them playing good shots or they are being bad sportspeople and verbally applying pressure, as long as you play the way you can and at your own speed, in your own time and in your own mind, you can come away feeling like you did all you could to win and either played better golf or showed that verbal pressure didn't work against you.

I will also reiterate here that only your swing is what you should be focusing on. Be better than your opponent by ignoring their bad behaviour or their personal way of playing.

Another form of pressure is during a busy period on the course. During busy times, you will always find the course will play a little slower because of the many groups teeing off before followed by the many groups teeing off after.

When this happens, and you're caught behind a slow group or the group in front of them are holding up play, you can often feel under pressure to rush your shots when you start seeing the group behind coming to the tee box. You and your group haven't done anything wrong. You're waiting to play your next shots, but can't, and the group behind can't play theirs, so when it comes to your turn to play, you just want to hit and move on. You lose out on taking your time, you aren't relaxed and you have a bad shot. Overcome this by ignoring the group behind when playing your shot.

If it's your group holding up play, again, don't feel like you have to rush your shot. Let the other players who are holding everything up feel the pressure and you take your time to play your shots as normal.

Finally, the pressure to score well. This is always a mindset that will impact your golf. As stated earlier in the chapter, don't focus on scoring until each hole is finished, and don't total up until each round has finished. Normal stroke play, hitting the fewest shots per hole, is the aim of the game. If you have a bad shot or hole, it adds pressure to the next shot or tee shot, and this will also impact scores. We come back to the current shot focus. Forget the bad shot or hole.

Relieve the pressure to need to score well on the remaining holes to have a great round. Continue to play one shot at a time, and over time, the shots will be better and the scores will naturally come down.

The last topic of this chapter is nerves. We all get nervous. It's natural for our mind and body to react to new environments (ie. A course you've never played before) or around new people (ie. Players you've never played golf with before), so when facing these situations, as well as teeing off in front of an audience on the first tee, it makes sense to feel nervous. The best thing to do is to embrace it. Prove to yourself that you can overcome nerves by relaxing, focusing, following routines and hitting the ball like you know you can.

Any important shot, whether it be a tee shot that needs to be good to stay in contention for a competition or a match winning putt, will create a sensation in our minds and will result in our nerves overreacting to counteract the pressure you've suddenly come under.

Take deep breaths, focus the mind on a good shot memory, come back to the present and only setup to take the shot once you're relaxed and ready.

Golf is meant to be a slow and steady sport. You're supposed to take your time and relax.

Never rush your shot if you are distracted by something or someone, or feel under pressure from other people or playing situations. Don't rush if you're nervous or fear the worst will happen.

Wait until you are fully ready to go for it with confidence and positivity before starting your setup.

If you've already started to setup, and something impacts you being ready, take your time and step away, and start again.

You control the flow of your own golf – not anything or anybody else – so wait until everything is physically and mentally in the right place.

Enjoy the game for what you want to get out of it, not because you feel the need to hit big shots or get close to the hole under pressure. Only by playing your own way and keeping to your own abilities will your mind settle and get less distracted, improving your golf instead of impacting it.

Fundamental #9: Goal Setting and Note Taking

Achievements drive us to improve at anything and provide us with reward & recognition.

In golf, win a tournament and you'll be rewarded with a trophy or a medal, or maybe another form of prize.

If you're not already an established player at a club or society, playing well will get you recognized by other golfers and you'll become a social golfer.

They'll probably invite you to their group for a weekly round or into their team for a competition, if you're not already part of the social side.

> 'All successful people have a goal. No one can get anywhere unless he knows where he wants to go and what he wants to be or do.'
>
> Norman Vincent Peale

It takes a lot of golf and a long time to get to a place where you can put yourself in contention for individual or team competitions. If you're new to golf, lots of lessons and playing time will give you every chance in the future.

If you're an experienced player, you'll already feel you should have good chances, maybe had a win or 2 in the past, but something is now missing that lets you down at the most critical time.

So, it makes sense to have some goals to help improve these chances or improve your golf in general.

You should have simple, achievable goals for every round. Achieve a self-set goal and reward yourself at the end of the round. It could be something like 'I will score at least 2 pars per 9 holes' or 'I will not lose a ball or drop a shot this round'.

Be mindful to make sure that you set yourself goals that will not provide distractions or errant thoughts during your round though.

They should be set before you start and only reviewed and rewarded after you've finished. That way you will know how well to reward yourself once you've finished, and it won't impact your round or your scores.

Also keep in mind that if a goal is not achieved for that round, don't get disheartened. Keep it as a goal for the ongoing rounds until it is achieved. Some goals can be set for every round, until you have achieved them and you are confident you no longer need them.

Other goals should be set weekly or monthly, depending on how regularly you play.

Finally, you should set some annual goals too – 2 or 3 achievable goals that you expect to complete and will improve your golf.

For example, set yourself a reduction in handicap – how many shots would you like to bring it down by? Be optimistic, but also realistic. 5 shots lower for a mid-high handicapper is very ambitious and probably unobtainable, where lowering it by 2 shots could be optimistic, realistic and achievable. Alternatively, set it to the nearest whole number or below.

For more experienced and lower double-digit handicap players, maybe you'd like to get to single figures and play to it consistently, and a single digit player might want to get to scratch.

Another example is to hit a number of rounds below a certain score – for mid-high handicappers, aim for 90 on a round of 18 holes or 45 on a round of 9 holes. For lower handicappers, aim for even par or lower

Maybe it's possible to increase your playing time, and you'd like to set a goal to play or practice more – increase by 1 more round per week or month, or play twice and practice on the range once every week, for example.

Whatever it takes to improve your game, without impacting your lifestyle and family or work time, you will need a goal or several to get there.

Something else that helps to set and achieve goals for golf is taking notes of your shots as you go along and of your rounds once you've finished.

Remember the planning a round chapter, I mention having a small pad and pen handy for mapping each hole how you'd like to play it, this can also be used to note how each shot and hole was played.

You've mapped out a tee shot and an approach shot on a par 4. You check your plan and see that the tee shot is a 3-wood to give you an ideal approach if it goes well. You look at the hole on the day and nothing needs adapting, so you stick to your original plan (always factor in any additional changes that could be needed once on the course, 3D looks different to 2D – there could be an uphill or downhill from the tee which cannot be seen from the plan that possibly changes the initial distance, maybe the weather impacts the shot and brings a hazard into play, etc.).

You take the shot and it lands on or near your intended target area. When you get there and check your plan again, make a quick note of the tee shot result.

Recognise how well it went and any conditions that may have affected your shot (or any conditions that could have but didn't affect your shot, ie. wind direction, weather conditions, sound or visual distractions, etc.). Then put your notepad away until you've finished the hole.

Write down anything else for how you finished the hole once you're on the next tee box and waiting. How was the approach shot? Did you need to lay up? Did you need any other shots (wayward recovery, bunker exit, lost ball for example)? How many putts did it take to sink the ball?

Do this for every hole, however good or bad you are playing. After you've finished the round, quickly analyse your notes. What was good, what was bad. If you've played the course before, how different was each hole this time? Where do you need to improve? What needs a little bit more focus or a lot more focus?

And finally, what goals can you set for the next or future rounds?

Intel is knowledge, knowledge is power, and great power will bring great achievements.

FUNDAMENTAL #10: CLUB SELECTION

I know it seems simple and obvious to write about club selection, but I want to raise awareness of the difficulties that impact shots when choosing the wrong club for what, in your mind, you think is the right club.

Think back to the round planning chapter again and consider which clubs you use for each particular shot. The plan is there as a guide to help map the round, and it's there to make the decision-making process easier on the day, but what if the scenario changes as you reach a tee or approach shot?

What if you've planned a 220yd tee shot with a 3-wood but the landing zone is uphill and into the wind? The contingency is to take the driver.

You have a club in mind but there will always be a reason for a different selection of club at some point in the round.

Go with the plan unless there is a need for contingency, but be confident and trusting in your decision if you change it.

What contingencies could impact the change in club? The weather, the lie, the distance, maybe hazards in the landing area or maybe the need to change from approach to lay up.

Maybe you need height instead of distance if you have to go over an obstacle to get to a safer position, then you'd choose a higher lofted club that will get you to a new target area, and then you'd adapt the next club because you won't be where you originally intended for the original approach plan.

> 'Golf is the closest game to the game we call life. You get bad breaks from good shots; you get good breaks from bad shots - but you have to play the ball where it lies.

Bobby Jones

A good step to take to aid with choosing the right club is to track your distances throughout the year. A winter round will always have less ball flight and run than you would get on a warm spring or summer day, so the seasons have an impact on your club selection.

We all know some shots won't always go where we want them to, so using the right club to recover is also important. What's the best recovery shot? Which club will provide the safest outcome?

Seeing a pro to help judge distances and practicing the right swings for specific shots with specific clubs will be great for your confidence in club selection too.

Don't spend too long making a decision and once you have made a decision, stick with it.

Commit to it.

Normally your gut instinct is the right instinct.

Indecision is only going to impact your thoughts and increase the chance of a bad shot or outcome.

As per previous chapters, make a plan that you can mostly stick to, focus on the current shot only and follow your pre-shot routines with the only club that makes sense in that moment, and you'll know you've made the right decision.

Know your distances.

Know the swing you are going to take and know you're doing everything you can to produce the best result from your club selection.

As part of the club selection mindset, the next chapter will focus on the higher-lofted scoring clubs, and when they come into play.

FUNDAMENTAL #11: THE SCORING CLUBS

To finish each hole with the fewest shots possible requires the right club selection on your approach or around the green.

Again, I know I'm stating the obvious here, but this time I am focusing on the clubs to use when within 140yds to the middle of the green.

8-iron, 9-iron and wedges (pitching, gap, sand or lob) specifically – as they are known as the scoring clubs due to their requirement to hit the approach shot into the green and as close to the hole as possible.

If you cover most of a par 4 with the tee shot and you're left with a simple, straight shot (ie. no wind or hills to impact the result, flat lie, etc.) into the green, you've got a good chance of hitting the ball close with a lower iron. At this point, when focusing on a target, you choose the flag.

Your pre-shot routine and setup will be focused in the direction of the flag and you'll choose the scoring club that covers the estimated distance directly to the hole.

Remember to account for any bounce or roll, with additional carry in the warmer months and less bounce, carry or roll in the colder months.

Ideally, you're giving yourself the best chance at a birdie and no worse than a par if your scoring clubs pull off the outcome you've focused on.

If missing the green, and it's a simple chip or flop shot back onto the green, again it's the scoring clubs that you will use for the desired outcome, and to get as close to the hole as possible.

'A shot that goes in the cup is pure luck, but a shot to within two feet of the flag is skill.'

Bobby Jones

Short par 3's are great for using and/or practicing with scoring clubs. One shot off the tee or short grass gives you an opportunity to hit the target, or get close, and score low.

Knowing the position and distance needed to finish the hole using the scoring clubs will definitely help improve your scores and eventually work towards bringing your handicap down.

I will be focusing more on the importance of the short game in a later chapter.

SHOT SELECTION #1: PUTTING

I'm starting with putting for the shot selection chapters because it's the first piece of the puzzle when bringing scores down.

There is a common saying amongst golfers 'drive for show, putt for dough' and therefore I feel it's the most important shot, because it's down to putting to finish each hole and it's where matches are won or lost.

Unless you've done well enough to pitch or chip in from off the green, or sunk the ball from the approach or tee shot, then the putt is the last shot on each hole, so it's important to recognize that almost half of your score is down to the number of putts in the round.

> 'A good player who is a great putter is a match for any golfer. A great hitter who cannot putt is a match for no one.'
>
> **Ben Sayers**

It's a game within the game. It's the nemesis of all golfers because it always seems like a simple shot that is always difficult to master.

It can be the difference between winning or losing in matchplay, in a tournament or team competition. Make your putts and you'll score better, which is easier said than done, so you need to have a positive mentality about putting, to look forward to making the shot that will mostly be used to get the ball in the hole. It always feels good when you make a long putt for birdie or par, or even have the chance for birdie and par and give it a good go.

Love putting and you'll love improving your scores.

Learn how to putt the way that makes you feel the most comfortable. I'm not going to talk about how you swing the putter or how you stand to take the shot, that's for the pro to help with.

I want to help with the putting mindset.

You're on the green and all you've got to do is get the ball in the hole. It sounds so simple, so what makes it so difficult and frustrating?

There are so many things that make putting go wrong – pin position, distance, grain of the grass, green conditions and targeting. However, it's being positive and focused that can change everything.

It's all in the mind.

I once played a round with some friends and most of my putts were either going in or very close. I was having a very good day. A playing partner asked what I was doing to be putting so well and I said 'I'm just aiming my ball and swinging my club towards the hole'. She was amazed at how it could be so simple. She started doing the same and for the last 4 holes of a 9-hole round, she took her time, focused her mind on the hole and putted less than she normally would.

So, that's all it takes. Pre-shot routine, hole targeting, setup and swing away.

If you keep a positive mindset, take any distracting thoughts away, relax, don't overthink it, go for the hole not just to get it close, then you'll make more putts than you miss.

Of course, you still won't make all of them, but you will be more consistent.

There will always be courses where the greens are fast and others that are slow. They will either be contoured or flat, and uphill or downhill. You study your line. You pick a target and you go for it.

Too many people say 'I just want to get it close' or 'as long as it goes past, it's a good putt'. They are both good statements if you have gone for the hole with each putt, if you've done everything you can to find a line, got a feel for the distance and speed and taken your shot to sink it with focus and positivity, but it hasn't gone in.

They are not good statements if you're just trying to get it close and within a certain area around the hole to make it easy for the next putt – you won't reduce your putts and scores if you don't go for the hole and at least try to get it in for fewer shots on the hole.

It's a waste of an opportunity to score lower, and that's not the aim of the game.

Before a round, it's good to get a little practice in. Just hit a few short putts to give yourself some confidence and to get a feel for the greens (note: be aware that not all practice greens mimic the greens out on the course, so you're only doing this to build confidence and trust in your line reading and swing).

Once the short putts are accurate, take a few slightly longer putts, but make sure they are sinkable. The last thing you want on your mind is that you're putting badly in practice so it's going to be even worse during the round on the course.

You're not practicing to see what the course will be like. You're giving yourself the mindset you need when you get to putt on each hole.

Confidence and trust are very important for putting.

The less you think about it and just do it, the more confident you'll feel and the more trust you will have in your putting to make the ball fall in the hole in as few attempts as possible.

Take your time getting to the greens but once you're there, enjoy being there because you know you'll do everything you can to putt well, and bring those scores down.

Also remember to be calm and relaxed if the first putt doesn't make it. Don't get angry or frustrated, and don't think about why it missed. Go and mark the ball, walk away for a second before coming back to study the new line for the next putt and do your best to follow your putting process to make it at the 2nd attempt.

There is also nothing wrong with 3 putting a difficult green if you're confident on other holes where you are only taking 1 putt.

Put the 3-putt in your notes, then move onto the next hole and forget about it.

Dwelling on it on future holes or when you're on the next green will only make you overthink other putts. Every hole is different, every green is different so every putt will be different.

So, go out there to sink those putts with positivity and confidence, and start the process of bringing those scores down on the greens.

Next chapter, we'll focus on the importance of the short game and why it's the next step to better scores.

SHOT SELECTION #2: THE SHORT GAME

> 'The secret of golf is to turn three shots into two.'
>
> Bobby Jones

The short game – where shots are made to get close to, or in, the hole, from around or approaching the green.

A lot of golfers don't realise how important the short game is, or where the scoring clubs come into play here. For most golfers, it's a case of measuring the distance and hit the ball towards the green, but a smart golfer will use the opportunity to hit a target on the green, and this is where the short game makes a big difference.

If you have a good tee shot on a par 4, it's most likely you'll be able to reach the green in two, no more than 3 shots. For a par 5, a good tee shot will give the opportunity for a good lay-up and then a good approach into the green.

I discussed putting in the last chapter – the normal last shot to close out the hole. But what if you didn't have to putt out because your short game is so good, you can get the ball in the hole from off the green or get it so close, the natural result is a 'gimme' or the chance to pick up and count the final shot without sinking it?

The short game, whether it be a chip from the side of the green or a wedge from 100yds, should be where you reduce your shots. It's the 2nd to last shot if you leave yourself with that 1 putt opportunity after you've played it.

The focus of the short game is often in the mindset of a golfer as just a formality to get on the green – it's not seen as the next best shot to finishing the hole, with putting being the most obvious hole closing shot.

If you miss the green from the approach shot, you'll be left with a short shot to get close to the hole, so it makes sense to know the right short shot to play and when.

If the ground is flat and dry, it could even be a putt from off the green that gets you close to the hole to follow up with a putt when on the green.

If it's uphill, maybe sitting in rough or anything not flat and smooth, or too far out to putt, then the ideal shot would either be a bump and run (hard ground) or flop shot (best when ground is soft) from a lower lofted club to get the ball up and down and as close to the hole as possible.

If the approach is short but still quite far out, consider a long bump and run with a 3-wd or 5-wd. The high loft keeps it down, but also gives it a lot of distance to travel to get to the green if taken the same way as a chip shot.

Additionally, you'd need to take into consideration any hazards in or out of play, and take the best short shot that would avoid them but still get the ball as close as possible.

If a hazard does cause a concern, then more loft to get over or maybe a scoring club if you can keep it low and go around it to the green.

I said about enjoying putting and to look forward to it. Use the positive mentality of wanting to only putt once to add positive focus to the short game too. You want to enjoy playing the short chips or wedge shots just as much as you enjoy sinking the putt or getting the feeling of getting a low score.

When you're in the short game position and you're choosing to use a scoring club, target the pin. Your aim is to get as close as possible, maybe even giving it a chance to go directly into the hole. A chip and run will mean you need to pick a landing spot so the ball can run onto, or into, the hole. A wedge shot will be better for landing next to, or very near to, the hole, which means the up and down of a high loft will stop it moving too far onwards.

Practice the short game more than you practice tee shots. When at the driving range, make sure a lot of time is spent getting the short game prepared. It's OK to practice tee shots too, but they only get you so far from the tee and very rarely all the way into a short game position.

Also, by practicing short game shots, this gives you an advantage on par 3s. It's technically, mostly, a short game shot off the tee.

Consider visiting Par 3 courses in your area, or pitch and putt courses, to hone in on the short shots and still play a game at the same time.

When playing a round, you'll always have tee shots on every hole. You might not always need a chip or a wedge, but you should always have a mindset available in your mental repertoire so that when you need to play a short shot to the hole, you pick the right club, you pick the flag and/or pin as your target, you follow your pre-shot routine and setup and give it your best try to get the ball in the hole, or as close as possible, to lower your scores.

You'll be amazed at how capable you will become at short game shots and chips when you need them the most, if you always have the mentality and focus to go for the hole at every opportunity.

SHOT SELECTION #3: LAY-UP AND APPROACH SHOTS

The approach to the green is the 'go for it' shot. After a good tee shot, or good recovery from a bad tee shot, you should be in the approach shot position. Your next shot gets you to the green.

A positive mindset to go for it and make it, gives you the best chance of getting to the green with that one shot.

A long approach means a wider approach too.

If you're close to the green, then the margin for error should be less because you have a small approach area, where the margin for error gets bigger as you get further away.

For example, let's say your ball is about 50yds short of the green. Imagine that there are 2 lines coming away from it and going towards the green at separate angles (ie. one goes off to the left and the other goes off to the right, almost forming a triangle with the green in the middle).

Now imagine those same lines creating a bigger triangle when you're further out (maybe 100yds or 150yds), therefore creating a new margin for error, which grows as you get further away from the green.

Hitting the green is the outcome you need and want, but with a larger margin for error from a longer distance, it's easy to get distracted or have bad thoughts about the wrong result from the next shot, which could impact the outcome of the next shot.

Go through the fundamentals, follow your processes, commit to go for it and the outcome is more likely to be positive.

'A great shot is when you pull it off. A smart shot is when you don't have the guts to try it.'

Phil Mickelson

If it's a short approach, think back to the scoring club chapter. Low scores will come if you're focused but relaxed, know your clubs and distances, have planned your ideal shots, have countered for contingencies and positive in mind and body – thoughts and swing.

The lay-up is a strategic shot. Either it's a long hole and you won't reach with an approach shot, or you are blocked by hazards and need a better approach.

Laying up is a safe decision. Why take the risk of going wrong from distance, and adding unnecessary shots to the score, when you could end up the same or better off by laying up and taking 2 safe shots instead?

Maybe laying up is unintentional. Your only choice is a long fairway wood because you are either too far away to reach the green, or it's the only club choice. You can do everything right, but end up short. This is not a bad shot or outcome, it just means an extra shot is needed, either a new approach with your scoring clubs, or if you're close enough, a putt from off the green to get the ball close to, or in, the hole.

Positivity and commitment are also required for the lay up shot. You need to measure the right distance to keep the ball safe, define the lay-up target and choose the right club for the shot.

A good lay-up will be used to give you the ideal approach shot, so maybe consider it in your round planning, in case you need it to help with getting to the ideal distance for your shot into the green.

Conservative and strategic golf, when needed, will be another string on the bow when it comes to playing the right shots that help reduce scores.

Use these to your advantage, and have the most positive mindset when you do.

Shot Selection #4: Tee Shots

The start of each hole. You can't move forwards until you've taken that first shot off the tee.

Very pinnacle to a good hole, a good tee shot will always give you the best chance to finish with a low score. Even a bad tee shot, left or right, too long or too short, in a hazard or in trees, can be recovered from, but essentially it should cover as much distance as possible, or as needed, and finish in a good, safe place, leaving the ball in an ideal location for approach or lay-up.

> 'You know what they say about big hitters... the woods are full of them.'
>
> Jimmy Demaret

The tee shot covers most, if not all, of the fundamentals in this book. Confidence, commitment and trust. Fear and pressure. Target setting and focus. Playing the only shot that matters at that point.

Planning the round gives you an idea of which club to use – remember, you don't always have to take the driver off the tee.

The most common bad memories come from tee shots, either from a previous hole in the same round or if playing a hole on a course you've played before, where it didn't go well last time around.

But you will also have some good memories of when you hit an awesome drive which brings back the positive feeling that you can do it again.

That's the mindset you need on every tee box. Remember what you CAN do from the tee, don't think about what you don't want to do.

Ideally, you'd only have 1 tee shot per hole, so keep it positive, trust in your swing and clubs.

Par 3 tee shots are like the approach shot. They are mostly short shots to the green. The closer you are, the lower the margin for error is when going for the green. Your tee shot focus and mentality is to keep the ball between two imaginary lines leading from the tee box to either side of the green (similar to the imaginary lines described chapter 15). The objective is to keep it within those imaginary lines and to target the flag and/or pin, to get it on the green first time.

Longer par 3 tee shots increase the risk of missing the green, so your mind opens up more to the possibility it'll go wrong. Overcome this by making sure you trust your swing mechanics and clubs for the shot you're playing and only play the shot when you feel ready and confident you can hit the green.

Par 5 tee shots are for position and distance. They are long holes, so you will always feel the need to hit the ball harder to get it to go further, but it's not always force that's needed, just the confidence that you have the technique and use the club to do the work. Too much force, or faster backswings than usual, will increase the risk of a bad outcome. Stick to your routine for any tee shot and let the clubs make it happen. Also, be decisive and not hesitant. If you don't need to use the driver to get into a good lay-up position, and you're more positive and confident with a wood or driving iron, go with your gut feel or planned club. Eliminate the risk to eliminate wasted shots. Be prepared for contingencies though. Be ready to adapt your mind to a change in decision, only if needed.

Finally, the most common length of hole is of course the par 4. These holes give you more chances to be adaptive to club selection for each tee shot.

Maybe you'd prefer to hit a long iron off the tee that could leave you with an approach with a wood or the same long iron. A par 4 tee shot is to help you land in a place that gives you the best approach for the 2nd shot. You don't have to overthink a par 4 tee shot because you aim for a certain place on a fairway, and not entirely looking to hit it a long way.

Use your planning, find your targets and make the most of the tee shot for position over distance on par 4s.

You will always feel more pressure from tee shots than any other shot, even putting. So many thoughts go through your head before, during and after your tee shots. The best mentality to have when taking tee shots is confidence. Only one thought should go through your mind and that is 'I can do this'. Then go through your pre-shot routine and setup and switch off to make the best tee shots that you can.

Start each hole on a high and your scores will go low.

SHOT SELECTION #5: BUNKER SHOTS

It makes sense to avoid bunkers whenever possible, but sometimes they just cannot be avoided. Sooner or later an errant shot or a bad bounce will cause the ball to land in the sand. It can be frustrating and disappointing to end up in a bunker, but it should not be detrimental to your game or score. The trick is knowing the right club, shot, stance and setup to get it out first time.

Bunker shots need practice. It is not the most common shot in the round, you might land in them once or twice per 18 holes, more if you're very unlucky, so they take some getting used to and being prepared for what you will face will help with the mindset and mentality.

Once you know how to escape them with little impact to your score, you'll never fear them or find them frustrating again.

Fairway bunkers are normally quite long and shallow. They're meant to cause a distraction to your tee shots or lay-ups. The best mentality is to ignore them. If you're planning the round and know your lines and distances, they shouldn't come into play as you'll be taking your shot to land away from them, but when it does happen, be mindful to ignore it. It's happened, it cannot be changed, so be committed and confident of getting it out first time.

'If profanity had an influence on the flight of the ball, the game of golf would be played far better than it is.'

Horace G Hutchinson

Playing out of a shallow fairway bunker is much the same as an approach or lay-up shot, because you want 2 things from the outcome – to get out and to land with an ideal next shot.

Club choice will come from knowing where you want to land – lofted clubs recommended to help with the height needed to clear any obstacles on the way out. You'll be hitting the ball with a full swing so judging distance and direction are vital to the setup process. The stance is just as important – you'll be slightly open-stance compared to a normal shot, to allow for the club to swing through, and the club face will need to be slightly more open than normal, to get a little more loft. Commitment and follow through are important to the swing process too.

Take some practice swings outside of the bunker before stepping in and setting up. I recommend getting a lesson or 2 on bunker shots, stance, swing and setup.

Your mind needs to avoid bad thoughts and your focus should be on ball connection and follow through. Visualise in your mind the right shot you want, then swing the same as your visualization. Be positive, committed and confident.

Greenside bunkers play much the same, but will require a few adaptations. However, your mindset and focus should never change, whichever bunker you're playing from.

Club selection is often the sand wedge, or your lowest lofted club, and your swing will be short, steady and committed again. You're not aiming for distance but for accuracy and proximity to the hole.

Open the stance a bit more than you would for a fairway bunker, and open the club face a bit more too. The last adaptation is to swing downwards and a couple of inches behind the ball instead of at the ball, to make connection with the sand first.

Stance, setup, swing and follow through are the vital components to keep in mind. Get those down to a tee (sorry, pun intended) and you'll be mentally prepared any time you miss the green and go into a greenside bunker instead.

Often, you'll find the bunker too deep, or the ball up against the front or back lip and you don't have a forwards shot.

The only change here is direction. Aim sideways or to the nearest safe location. Save yourself any wasted shots from the same bunker by playing safe, confident that you know your next shot will get you on, or closer, to the green.

Don't take any unnecessary risks out of bunkers.

Reduce any chance of impacting your confidence as well as your score.

With bunkers – practice, practice, practice.

FINAL CHAPTER: PRACTICE AND LESSONS

I tell my children that practice makes you better, because nothing can ever be perfect, especially in golf. No shot is ever the same and being perfect wouldn't leave any room for improvement, and it's more likely you'd start going backwards in your game rather than forwards.
We want forwards momentum and continuous improvement. We're not searching for perfection, only to keep getting better.

Practice is not just about making your swing better but also your mindset and mentality.

Practicing certain shots on the practice green or driving range will build your confidence ready for when you face that shot on the course.

Being prepared for what shots will come allows you to have the right mindset for when the shot does come.

> **'Without continued growth and progress, such words as improvement, achievement and success have no meaning.'**
>
> **Benjamin Franklin**

However, beware that over-practicing can also cause bad habits to creep into your mechanics or confidence to go down, if the practice shots don't go as well as hoped, so only practice what you need to, and move onto another club or stop once you've got the shot right for you.

A good tip for the driving range is to alternate clubs for each shot and use your pre-shot routine and setup as if you were on the course.

Don't use one club for the whole session, or for all the practice balls. Set a number of balls aside for a certain club then practice some on-the-course shots – tee then approach, or approach and chip, or tee then lay-up followed by approach, for example.

There are many driving ranges using technology these days, with more and more courses installing new systems. I recommend finding your nearest course with new technology, so you're not just hitting a ball at the range, but possibly playing a virtual course or aiming into targets.

It's from here that you could move onto lessons with the pro. Define your weaknesses, where you need to improve or change something wrong, and find the right pro who will listen to you and help you. Build a relationship with the pro. They will be able to guide you better if they know who you are as a person and not just as a golfer. They'll be more value for money if they can help your mentality and not just your swing mechanics.

Once you've had enough range lessons, make sure the pro is available for on-course lessons too. You'll be putting what you've learnt from your range lessons into action when playing on the course in between lessons, but it will be to your advantage to have the pro follow you round to make sure you're continuing to play with what you've learnt.

If you need more confidence with putting, or just need to get those close putts in more regularly, learn some drills to take onto the practice greens. Start off close, then work your way outwards, or give yourself a smaller target, like a tee, so that when going for the hole, it's naturally a bigger target.

Practice bunker shots and your short game, pitching and chipping to aim for the hole from off the green. Treat every round as a practice round and treat every practice as if you're playing on a course.

Success comes from repetition, so you will grow confident with more practice.

Life is busy – friends and family commitments, work commitments or playing other sports often mean there is less time to practice or have lessons, so make every opportunity count.

Learn from mistakes, keep notes so that you have a goal when practicing, not just every time you go out on the course but on the range or practice areas too.

Improvement will come if you're committed to mind and body practice time. Use the fundamentals in this book to aid in your practice, as well as in your competitions and team efforts, and take advantage of the following templates and quick-thoughts pullout every time you play or practice.

You've now reached the 19th Hole, it's been a long time coming, so make time to enjoy a well-deserved drink for reading this book and taking it all in.

EPILOGUE

'No matter how good you get, you can always get better - and that's the exciting part.'

Tiger Woods

Whether you're an experienced golfer or a beginner, I have written this book from a fellow golfer's perspective in hope that you'll take at least one thing, if not many things, away from what I have included and use what you've learnt when out on the course or on the practice areas.

To the experienced golfer, a lot of what I've written will be obvious, but hopefully there is something missing from your game that this book will help with or bring back a memory of something you've forgotten.

For beginners, hopefully it will help you learn how your mindset is just as important as your swing mechanics or how you hit the ball. You will learn something new or become aware of something that will aid in your improvement.

Opening your eyes, and mind, to the multiple impacts that having the correct mindset and mentality has on the game of golf will help you improve one step at a time.

Golf is not just physically tiring, because of the miles walked carrying a bag or pulling a trolley, or even if using a buggy, but it is also mentally tiring.

Changing the mindset to decrease frustration and overthinking will reduce the mental tiredness at the end of a round.

Keeping the mind focused on each shot and switching off from distractions and errant thoughts means you are limiting how much you think throughout the round too, allowing for more relaxation in between shots.

Two of my favourite quotes of all time come from Albert Einstein and they are a great inspiration to golf mentality, so I'm going to end this book with them and hopefully they will inspire you too.

1. **'A person who never made a mistake never tried anything new'**
2. **'The definition of insanity is doing the same thing over and over and expecting different results'**

Play Golf! Love Golf! THINK LESS! Golf!

- Don't forget the purpose of golf – to put the ball in the hole in as fewer shots as possible
- Plan your round from green to tee – ideal shot distances – plan your actions so you can action your plans
- Keep your focus on one shot at a time – the one you're about to play. Forget any previous shots and don't think about any future shots.
- Always have a small target, visually and in your mind. See where you want the ball to go. Have a distant target for long shots and a local target for putts or greenside shots.
- Always follow your pre-shot and setup routines.
- Approximately only 10% of any round is spent hitting the ball. Keep relaxed but focused for the other 90%.
- Be confident, be committed and trust your swing, your clubs and, most importantly, yourself.
- Be positive and be resilient. Don't let anything get in the way of good golf.
- Avoid distractions whenever possible. If distracted, reset yourself.
- Eliminate fear, relieve any pressure you might feel and embrace any nerves.
- Make goals and stick to them to achieve them

- Make notes of your round. Analyse at the end of the round or when you get home. Never analyse a shot during the round. Make a note and forget about it.

- Go with your gut instinct for club selection. You know your distances and capabilities. If in doubt, keep the ball in play. Avoid going longer than you need to.

- Always factor in uncontrolled circumstances – weather, bad lies, bad bounces and bad outcomes. They happen, so take the next shot knowing there was nothing you can do to change them.

- Practice as much as possible, but be mindful to alternate the shots you practice.

- Make putting and short game practice a priority whenever possible. Matches are won and rounds are scored low when scoring clubs and putters are used.

- Get lessons if you feel uncomfortable about a shot, unconfident of a club or if you are a beginner. Commit to learn and learn to commit.

- Only you have the influence on how well you do, so do your best to be the best you can.

ROUND PLANNING TEMPLATES

(PRINT OR COPY, TO READ THROUGHOUT THE ROUND OR PRACTICE)

Hole	Par	yds	S.I.
# of shots given			
Tee shot Club:			
Lay-up Club:			
Approach Club:			
# of Putts:			

Notes

Hole	Par	yds	S.I.
# of shots given			
Tee shot Club:			
Lay-up Club:			
Approach Club:			
# of Putts:			

Notes

ROUND PLANNING TEMPLATES

(PRINT OR COPY, TO READ THROUGHOUT THE ROUND OR PRACTICE)

Hole	Par	yds	S.I.
# of shots given			
Tee shot Club:			
Lay-up Club:			
Approach Club:			
# of Putts:			

Notes

Hole	Par	yds	S.I.
# of shots given			
Tee shot Club:			
Lay-up Club:			
Approach Club:			
# of Putts:			

Notes

ACKNOWLEDGEMENTS

I couldn't have written this book were it not for my friends and family who support my love of golf.

Golf is a very time-consuming sport, so it means being away from home for lots of, and long, periods of time.

I thank my wife Clare for her patience and support when I take the time to have a round at the club with friends or for competitions and I'm not able to spend that time with our children.

I also thank my children, Dexter and Felicity, for supporting Clare while I am out playing a sport I really enjoy.

Next, I'd like to thank my friend and fellow golfer, Simon Taylor.

Despite being busy with his own company, spending time with his family and out playing golf, he has taken the time to read my first draft and challenge my writing by letting me know where things look great or what needed some adapting. I hope some of my advice has helped his game since.

Also, another fellow golfer and family friend, Steve Kennedy. A single-digit handicap player with lots of experience and a PGA pro brother.

Between travelling with his family, playing golf and starting a new job, he was able to read through and provide advice on any changes that needed making and where he found it to remind him of the bits of detail that he had forgotten had gotten him to how he plays today.

Finally, there was always going to be an inspiration from somewhere and this came from reading similar mental guidance golf books, and I recommend reading/buying any books by US sports psychologist Dr Bob Rotella.

As an amateur golfer, I don't spend as much time on the course or at the driving range as I would like. Reading his books highlight a lot about how the pros became who they are today, how they changed their mindset to go from mediocre to great players and win tournaments.

I took this onboard but I have viewed it from the perspective of an amateur who can't play or practice for hours every day and my words in this book are to help other amateurs get better and realise their own potential too.

Lastly, thank you to you for buying this book and I hope you take at least one part of it that improves your mindset and the way you: Play golf! Love golf! Think less! Golf!

ENGLAND
TICK THE COURSES YOU'VE PLAYED...

GOLF COURSE DIRECTORY: ENGLAND

Bedfordshire

- Aylesbury Vale ○
- Bedford & County ○
- Bedfordshire ○
- Caddington ○
- Cainhoe Wood ○
- Chalgrave Manor ○
- Colworth & North Beds ○
- Dunstable Downs ○
- Henlow ○
- Ivinghoe ○
- John O'Gaunt ○
- Leighton Buzzard ○
- Luton Hoo Hotel ○
- Mount Pleasant ○
- Mowsbury ○
- Pavenham Park ○
- Sharnbrook ○
- South Beds ○
- Stockwood Park ○
- The Millbrook ○
- Tilsworth ○
- Wyboston Lakes ○

Berkshire

- Bearwood Lakes ○
- Billingbear Park ○
- Bird Hills ○
- Bradfield College ○
- Calcot Park ○
- Castle Royle ○
- Datchet ○
- Deanwood Park ○
- Donnington Grove ○
- Donnington Valley ○
- East Berkshire ○
- Easthampstead ○
- Eton College ○
- Fernhill Artisans ○
- Goring & Streatley ○
- Hennerton ○
- Maidenhead ○
- Mill Ride ○
- Newbury & Crookham ○
- Royal Ascot ○
- Royal Household ○
- Sand Martins ○
- Sonning ○
- Sunningdale ○
- Sunningdale Heath ○
- Temple ○
- The Berkshire ○
- The Caversham ○
- The Club at Mapledurham ○
- The Downshire ○
- The West Berkshire ○
- Theale ○
- Wellington College ○
- Winter Hill ○
- Wokefield Park ○

GOLF COURSE DIRECTORY: ENGLAND

Bristol

- Bristol & Clifton
- Clevedon
- Filton
- Knowle
- Mendip Spring
- Shirehampton Park
- The Bristol
- The Players
- Tickenham
- Woodlands
- Chipping Sodbury
- Farrington
- Henbury
- Long Ashton
- Saltford
- Stockwood Vale
- The Kendleshire
- Thornbury
- Tracy Park
- Woodspring

Buckinghamshire

- Abbey Hill
- Beaconsfield
- Buckinghamshire
- Chartridge Park
- Chiltern Forest
- Ellesborough
- Flackwell Heath
- Harewood Downs
- Hazlemere
- Huntswood
- Oakland Park
- Richings Park
- Stowe
- The South Buckinghamshire
- Thorney Park
- Wexham Park
- Windmill Hill
- Wycombe Heights
- Aspley Guise/Woburn Sands
- Buckingham
- Burnham Beeches
- Chesham & Ley Hill
- Denham
- Farnham Park
- Gerrards Cross
- Harleyford
- Hedsor
- Iver
- Princes Risborough
- Silverstone
- The Lambourne
- The Three Locks
- Weston Turville
- Whiteleaf
- Woburn

GOLF COURSE DIRECTORY: ENGLAND

Cambridgeshire

- March ○
- Cambridge Country ○
- Elton Furze ○
- Girton ○
- Lakeside Lodge ○
- Oundle ○
- Ramsey ○
- St Neots ○
- The Gog Magog ○
- Thorney Lakes ○
- Brampton Park ○
- Cambridge Meridian ○
- Ely City ○
- Kingsway ○
- Nene Park ○
- Peterborough Milton ○
- St Ives (Cambs) ○
- The Cambridgeshire ○
- The Old Nene ○

Channel Islands

- Alderney ○
- La Moye ○
- Les Mielles ○
- Royal Guernsey ○
- St Clements ○
- Wheatlands ○
- Le Grande Mare ○
- L'ancresse ○
- Les Ormes ○
- Royal Jersey ○
- St Pierre Park ○

Cheshire

- Alder Root ○
- Aldersey Green ○
- Antrobus ○
- Arrowe Park ○
- Astbury ○
- Bidston ○
- Brackenwood ○
- Bramhall ○
- Caldy ○
- Cheadle ○
- Congleton ○
- Davenport ○
- Disley ○
- Eastham Lodge ○
- Alderley Edge ○
- Altrincham ○
- Arderne (Portal) ○
- Ashton-on-Mersey ○
- Avro ○
- Birchwood ○
- Bramall Park ○
- Bromborough ○
- Carden Park ○
- Chester ○
- Crewe ○
- Delamere Forest ○
- Dunham Forest ○
- Eaton ○

Cheshire (cont...)

- Ellesmere Port ○
- Hale ○
- Hazel Grove ○
- Helsby ○
- Heyrose ○
- Hooton Ladies ○
- Irby ○
- Leasowe ○
- Lymm ○
- Malkins Bank ○
- Mellor & Townscliffe ○
- Mottram Hall ○
- Onneley ○
- Poulton Park ○
- Prestbury ○
- Queens Park ○
- Ringway ○
- Royal Liverpool ○
- Sale ○
- Sandiway ○
- Stamford ○
- Styal ○
- The Shrigley Hall ○
- The Wilmslow ○
- Upton by Chester ○
- Vicars Cross ○
- Walton Hall ○
- Wellington ○
- Widnes ○
- Wychwood Park ○
- Gatley ○
- Hartford ○
- Heaton Manor ○
- Heswall ○
- High Legh Park ○
- Hoylake ○
- Knutsford ○
- Leigh ○
- Macclesfield ○
- Marple ○
- Mersey Valley ○
- Northop ○
- Portal ○
- Prenton ○
- Pryors Hayes ○
- Reddish Vale ○
- Romiley ○
- Runcorn ○
- Sandbach ○
- St Helens ○
- Stockport ○
- The Mere ○
- The Tytherington Club ○
- The Wirral ○
- Vale Royal Abbey ○
- Wallasey ○
- Warrington ○
- West Hoyle ○
- Woodside ○

GOLF COURSE DIRECTORY: ENGLAND

Cornwall

- Bowood Park Hotel ○
- Budock Vean ○
- Carlyon Bay ○
- Falmouth ○
- Lanhydrock Hotel ○
- Looe ○
- Mullion ○
- Perranporth ○
- Radnor ○
- St Enodoc ○
- St Mellion ○
- The Point at Polzeath ○
- Trethorne ○
- Truro ○
- Whitsand Bay ○
- Bude & North Cornwall ○
- Cape Cornwall ○
- China Fleet ○
- Isles of Scilly ○
- Launceston ○
- Merlin ○
- Newquay ○
- Porthpean ○
- St Austell ○
- St Kew ○
- Tehidy Park ○
- Treloy ○
- Trevose ○
- West Cornwall ○

County Durham

- Barnard Castle ○
- Billingham ○
- Bishop Auckland ○
- Brancepeth Castle ○
- Chester-Le-Street ○
- Crook ○
- Dinsdale ○
- Eaglescliffe ○
- Headlam Hall ○
- Ingleby Barwick ○
- Oakleaf ○
- Rockliffe Hall ○
- Seaham ○
- Sharpley Springs ○
- Teesside ○
- Woodham
- Beamish Park ○
- Birtley Portobello ○
- Blackwell Grange ○
- Castle Eden ○
- Consett & District ○
- Darlington ○
- Durham City ○
- Hartlepool ○
- Ineos ○
- Knotty Hill ○
- Ramside Hall Hotel ○
- Roseberry Grange Community ○
- Seaton Carew ○
- South Moor ○
- The Wynyard Club ○

GOLF COURSE DIRECTORY: ENGLAND

Cumbria

Alston Moor	○	Appleby	○
Barrow	○	Carlisle	○
Carus Green	○	Casterton	○
Cockermouth	○	Eden	○
Eskdale	○	Furness	○
Grange Fell	○	Grange Over Sands	○
Kendal	○	Keswick	○
Kirkby Lonsdale	○	Maryport	○
Penrith	○	Seascale	○
Sedbergh	○	Silecroft	○
Silloth on Solway	○	St Bees	○
Stony Holme	○	The Dunnerholme	○
Ulverston	○	Whitehaven	○
Windermere	○	Workington	○

Derbyshire

Alfreton	○	Ashbourne	○
Bakewell	○	Barlborough Links	○
Brailsford	○	Broughton Heath	○
Burton-on-Trent	○	Buxton & High Peak	○
Cavendish	○	Chapel-en-le-Frith	○
Chatsworth	○	Chesterfield	○
Chevin	○	Derby	○
Erewash Valley	○	Glossop	○
Hallowes	○	Hope	○
Horsley Lodge	○	Kedleston Park	○
Marriott Breadsall Priory	○	Matlock	○
Mickleover	○	Morley Hayes	○
New Mills	○	Ormonde Fields	○
Pastures	○	Shirland	○
Sickleholme	○	South Chesterfield	○
Stanedge	○	Tapton Park	○

GOLF COURSE DIRECTORY: ENGLAND

Devon

Ashbury	○	Axe Cliff	○
Bigbury	○	Boringdon	○
Bovey Castle	○	Bovey Tracey	○
Churston	○	Dainton Park	○
Dartmouth Hotel	○	Downes Crediton	○
East Devon	○	Elfordleigh	○
Exeter	○	Exminster	○
Fingle Glen	○	Great Torrington	○
Holsworthy	○	Honiton	○
Ilfracombe	○	Ivybridge	○
Libbaton	○	Lion Artisan	○
Mortehoe & Woolacombe	○	Okehampton	○
Portmore	○	Royal North Devon	○
Saunton	○	Sidmouth	○
Staddon Heights	○	Stover	○
Tavistock	○	Teign Valley	○
Teignmouth	○	The Mole Resort	○
Thurlestone	○	Tiverton	○
Torquay	○	Welbeck Manor	○
Woodbury Park Hotel	○	Yelverton	○

Dorset

Bournemouth & Meyrick Park	○	Bridport & West Dorset	○
Broadstone	○	Bulbury Woods	○
Came Down	○	Canford School	○
Christchurch	○	Crane Valley	○
Dorset	○	Dudsbury	○
Ferndown	○	Ferndown Forest	○
Folke	○	Highcliffe Castle	○
Isle of Purbeck	○	Knighton Heath	○
Lyme Regis	○	Merley Park	○
Moors Valley	○	Parkstone	○
Parley Court	○	Queens Park	○
Remedy Oak	○	Sherborne	○
Somerley Park	○	Sturminster Marshall	○

Dorset (cont...)

The Ashley Wood	○	Wareham	○
Weymouth	○	Wolfedale	○

East Sussex

Ashdown Park	○	Beauport Park	○
Boars Head	○	Brighton & Hove	○
Cooden Beach	○	Crowborough Beacon	○
Dale Hill Hotel	○	Dyke	○
East Brighton	○	East Sussex National	○
Eastbourne Downs	○	Highwoods	○
Hollingbury Park	○	Horam Park	○
Lewes	○	Mid Sussex	○
Peacehaven	○	Piltdown	○
Royal Ashdown Forest	○	Royal Eastbourne	○
Rye	○	Seaford	○
Seaford Head	○	Sedlescombe	○
The Lottbridge	○	Wellshurst	○
West Hove	○	Willingdon	○

East Yorkshire

Beverley & East Riding	○	Boothferry	○
Bridlington	○	Bridlington Links	○
Brough	○	Burstwick Country	○
Cave Castle	○	Cottingham Parks	○
Driffield	○	Far Grange Park	○
Flamborough Head	○	Ganstead Park	○
Hainsworth Park	○	Hessle	○
Hornsea	○	Hull	○
Skidby Lakes	○	Springhead Park	○
Sutton Park	○	Withernsea	○

Essex

Abridge	○	Ballards Gore	○
Basildon	○	Belfairs	○
Belhus Park	○	Bentley	○
Benton Hall	○	Birch Grove	○
Blakes	○	Boyce Hill	○
Braintree	○	Braxted Park	○
Brentwood	○	Burnham-on-Crouch	○
Canons Brook	○	Castle Point	○
Chelmsford	○	Chigwell	○
Clacton-on-Sea	○	Colchester	○
Colne Valley	○	Crondon Park	○
Crowlands Heath	○	Epping	○
Five Lakes	○	Forrester Park	○
Frinton	○	Garon Park	○
Golf World Stansted	○	Gosfield Lake	○
Hainault Forest	○	Hartswood	○
Harwich & Dovercourt	○	Ingrebourne Links	○
Langdon Hills	○	Lexden Wood	○
Maldon	○	Mardyke Valley	○
Maylands	○	Millers Barn	○
Nazeing	○	Orsett	○
Risebridge	○	Rivenhall Oaks	○
Rochford Hundred	○	Romford	○
Saffron Walden	○	Stapleford Abbotts	○
Stock Brook	○	Stoke by Nayland Hotel	○
The Burstead	○	The Essex	○
The Heron	○	The Notleys	○
The Rayleigh Club	○	The Warren	○
Theydon Bois	○	Thorndon Park	○
Thorpe Hall	○	Three Rivers	○
Top Meadow	○	Upminster	○
Warley Park	○	Woolston Manor	○

Gloucestershire

- Brickhampton ○
- Cirencester ○
- Cleeve Hill ○
- Cotswold Edge ○
- Cotswold Hills ○
- Dymock Grange ○
- Forest Hills ○
- Forest of Dean ○
- Gloucester ○
- Lilley Brook ○
- Lydney ○
- Minchinhampton ○
- Naunton Downs ○
- Painswick ○
- Puckrup Hall Hotel ○
- Rodway Hill ○
- Sherdons ○
- South Cerney ○
- StarGolf ○
- Stinchcombe Hill ○
- The Bells Hotel & Country ○
- Tp Golf Tewkesbury Park ○
- Westonbirt ○

Greater Manchester

- Ashton-in-Makerfield ○
- Blackley ○
- Brookdale ○
- Castle Hawk ○
- Chorlton Cum Hardy ○
- Davyhulme Park ○
- Denton ○
- Didsbury ○
- Dukinfield ○
- Ellesmere ○
- Fairfield ○
- Flixton ○
- Gathurst ○
- Haigh Hall ○
- Heaton Park ○
- Hindley Hall ○
- Houldsworth ○
- Manchester ○
- Marland, Springfield Park ○
- Marriott Worsley Park ○
- North Manchester ○
- Northenden ○
- Pennington ○
- Prestwich ○
- Rochdale ○
- Saddleworth ○
- Stand ○
- Tunshill ○
- Werneth Low ○
- Whitefield ○
- Whittaker ○
- Wigan ○
- Withington ○
- Worsley ○

Hampshire

Alresford	○	Alton	○
Ampfield	○	Andover	○
Army	○	Avington Park	○
Barton-on-Sea	○	Basingstoke	○
Bishopswood	○	Blackmoor	○
Blacknest	○	Blackwater Valley	○
Boundary Lakes	○	Bramshaw	○
Bramshott Hill	○	Brokenhurst Manor	○
Cams Hall Estate	○	Chilworth	○
Corhampton	○	East Horton	○
Fleetlands	○	Gosport & Stokes	○
Hartley Wintney	○	Hayling	○
Hockley	○	Leckford	○
Lee-on-the-Solent	○	Liphook	○
Meon Valley	○	New Forest	○
North Hants	○	Old Thorns	○
Paultons	○	Petersfield	○
Portsmouth	○	Romsey	○
Rowlands Castle	○	Royal Winchester	○
Sandford Springs	○	Sherfield Oaks	○
Skylark	○	South Winchester	○
Southampton Municipal	○	Southsea	○
Southwick Park	○	Stoneham	○
Test Valley	○	The Burley	○
The Hampshire	○	Tournerbury	○
Tylney Park	○	Walhampton	○
Waterlooville	○	Wellow	○
Weybrook Park	○	Wickham Park	○
Worldham	○		

Herefordshire

Alexander Park Resort	○	Burghill Valley	○
Halo	○	Kington	○
Ross-on-Wye	○	South Herefordshire	○
The Herefordshire	○		

GOLF COURSE DIRECTORY: ENGLAND

Hertfordshire

- Aldenham ○
- Arkley ○
- Ashridge ○
- Batchwood Hall ○
- Berkhamsted ○
- Brickendon Grange ○
- Centurion ○
- Cheshunt Park ○
- Dyrham Park ○
- Essendon ○
- Hadley Wood ○
- Harpenden ○
- Hartsbourne Country Club ○
- Knebworth ○
- Little Hay ○
- Mid Herts ○
- Moor Park ○
- Panshanger ○
- Redbourn ○
- Royston ○
- Stevenage ○
- The Cheshunt ○
- The Hertfordshire ○
- The Melbourne ○
- Verulam ○
- West Herts ○
- Whitehill ○
- Aldwickbury Park ○
- Ash Valley ○
- Barkway Park ○
- Batchworth Park ○
- Bishops Stortford ○
- Brookmans Park ○
- Chesfield Downs ○
- Chorleywood ○
- East Herts ○
- Great Hadham ○
- Hanbury Manor ○
- Harpenden Common ○
- Heydon Grange ○
- Letchworth ○
- Manor of Groves Hotel ○
- Mill Green ○
- Old Ford Manor ○
- Porters Park ○
- Rickmansworth ○
- Shendish Manor ○
- Stocks ○
- The Grove ○
- The Hertsmere ○
- The Shire London ○
- Welwyn Garden City ○
- Whipsnade Park ○

Isle of Man

- Castletown ○
- Douglas ○
- Mount Murray ○
- Port St Mary ○
- Comis Hotel ○
- King Edward Bay ○
- Peel ○
- Rowany ○

Isle of Wight

Cowes	○	Freshwater Bay	○
Osborne	○	Ryde	○
Shanklin & Sandown	○	Ventnor	○
Westridge	○		

Kent

Ashford (Kent)	○	Barnehurst	○
Bearsted	○	Bexleyheath	○
Birchwood Park	○	Boughton	○
Bromley	○	Broome Park	○
Canterbury	○	Chart Hills	○
Chelsfield Lakes	○	Cherry Lodge	○
Chestfield	○	Chislehurst	○
Cobtree Manor Park	○	Corinthian	○
Dartford	○	Etchinghill	○
Faversham	○	Felixstowe Ferry	○
Gillingham	○	Hever Castle	○
High Elms	○	Holtye	○
Hythe	○	Kings Hill	○
Kingsnorth	○	Knole Park	○
Lamberhurst	○	Langley Park	○
Leeds Castle	○	Littlestone	○
London	○	London Beach	○
Lullingstone Park	○	Lydd	○
Manston	○	Marriott Tudor Park	○
Mid Kent	○	Nevill	○
Nizels	○	North Foreland	○
Orpington Cray Valley	○	Park Wood	○
Pedham Place	○	Poult Wood	○
Princes	○	Redlibbets	○
Rochester & Cobham	○	Royal Cinque Ports	○
Sene Valley	○	Sevenoaks Town	○
Sheerness	○	Sittingbourne & Milton Regis	○
St Augustines	○	Stonelees	○
Sundridge Park	○	Sweetwoods	○

Kent (cont…)

- Tenterden ○
- The Ridge ○
- Upchurch River Valley ○
- Weald of Kent ○
- West Malling ○
- Westgate & Birchington ○
- Wildernesse ○
- The Darenth ○
- The Royal St Georges ○
- Walmer & Kingsdown ○
- West Kent ○
- Westerham ○
- Whitstable & Seasalter ○
- Wrotham Heath ○

Lancashire

- Accrington & District ○
- Ashton-under-Lyne ○
- Baxenden & District ○
- Blackpool North Shore ○
- Bolton ○
- Breightmet ○
- Bury ○
- Clitheroe ○
- Crompton & Royton ○
- Dean Wood ○
- Douglas Valley ○
- Duxbury Park ○
- Fleetwood ○
- Great Harwood ○
- Green Haworth ○
- Hart Common ○
- Herons Reach ○
- Highfield ○
- Knott End ○
- Lansil ○
- Lobden ○
- Lowes Park ○
- Marsden Park ○
- Mossock Hall ○
- Mytton Fold ○
- Oak Royal ○
- Ashton & Lea ○
- Bacup ○
- Blackburn ○
- Blackpool Park ○
- Bolton Old Links ○
- Burnley ○
- Chorley ○
- Colne ○
- Darwen ○
- Deane ○
- Dunscar ○
- Fairhaven ○
- Ghyll ○
- Great Lever & Farnworth ○
- Greenmount ○
- Harwood ○
- Heysham ○
- Hurlston Hall ○
- Lancaster ○
- Leyland ○
- Longridge ○
- Lytham Green Drive ○
- Morecambe ○
- Myerscough ○
- Nelson ○
- Oldham ○

Lancashire (cont…)

- Ormskirk ○
- Pike Fold ○
- Poulton-Le-Fylde ○
- Regent Park ○
- Rossendale ○
- Shaw Hill Hotel ○
- Southport Academy ○
- Staining Lodge ○
- Towneley ○
- Walmersley ○
- Westhoughton ○
- Wilpshire ○
- Penwortham ○
- Pleasington ○
- Preston ○
- Rishton ○
- Royal Lytham & St Annes ○
- Silverdale ○
- Annes Old Links ○
- Stonyhurst Park ○
- Turton ○
- Werneth ○
- Whalley ○

Leicestershire

- Beedles Lake ○
- Charnwood Forest ○
- Forest Hill ○
- Hinckley ○
- Kibworth ○
- Kirby Muxloe ○
- Longcliffe ○
- Market Harborough ○
- Rothley Park ○
- Scraptoft ○
- The Leicestershire ○
- Whetstone ○
- Birstall ○
- Cosby ○
- Glen Gorse ○
- Humberstone Heights ○
- Kilworth Springs ○
- Lingdale ○
- Lutterworth ○
- Melton Mowbray ○
- Rushcliffe ○
- Six Hills ○
- Ullesthorpe Court Hotel ○
- Willesley Park ○

GOLF COURSE DIRECTORY: ENGLAND

Lincolnshire

- Ashby Decoy
- Belton Woods
- Boston
- Burghley Park
- Cleethorpes
- Forest Pines
- Grimsby
- Humberston
- Kirton Holme
- Lincoln
- Market Rasen
- Millfield
- North Shore Hotel
- RAF Coningsby
- Sleaford
- Southwell
- Stoke Rochford
- Sutton Bridge
- Thonock Park
- Toft
- Welton Manor
- Woodthorpe Hall
- Belton Park
- Blankney
- Boston West Country Park
- Carholme
- Elsham
- Gedney Hill
- Holme Hall
- Kenwick
- Laceby Manor
- Louth
- Messingham Grange
- Normanby Hall
- Pottergate
- Seacroft
- South Kyme
- Spalding
- Sudbrook Moor
- Tetney
- Thorpe Park
- Waltham Windmill
- Woodhall Spa

London

- Aquarius
- Bush Hill Park
- Dulwich & Sydenham Hill
- Finchley
- Hendon
- Ilford
- London Scottish
- Mitcham
- North Middlesex
- Richmond Park
- Royal Blackheath
- Brent Valley
- Chingford
- Eltham Warren
- Hampstead
- Highgate
- Leaside
- Mill Hill
- Muswell Hill
- Putney Park
- Roehampton
- Royal Epping Forest

London (cont…)

Royal Wimbledon ○
Shortlands ○
South Herts ○
Wanstead ○
West London ○
Woodford ○
Shooters Hill ○
Sidcup ○
Thetford ○
West Essex ○
Wimbledon Common ○

Merseyside

Allerton Manor ○
Berrington Hall ○
Bootle ○
Childwall ○
Formby Hall ○
Grange Park ○
Hesketh ○
Houghwood ○
Kirkby Valley ○
Park ○
Sherdley Park ○
Southport Golf Links ○
Warren Municipal ○
West Lancashire ○
Alt ○
Blundells Hill ○
Bowring ○
Formby ○
Grand National ○
Haydock Park ○
Hillside ○
Huyton & Prescot ○
Lee Park ○
Royal Birkdale ○
Southport & Ainsdale ○
Southport Old Links ○
West Derby ○
Woolton ○

Middlesex

Ashford Manor ○
David Lloyd Club Hampton ○
Enfield ○
Grims Dyke ○
Harrow School ○
Hillingdon ○
Perivale Park ○
Sandy Lodge ○
Stockley Park ○
Sudbury ○
Uxbridge ○
Wyke Green ○
Crews Hill ○
Ealing ○
Fulwell ○
Harefield Place ○
Haste Hill ○
Northwood ○
Pinner Hill ○
Stanmore ○
Strawberry Hill ○
Sunbury ○
West Middlesex ○

Norfolk

- Barnham Broom
- Bawburgh
- Caldecott Hall
- Denver
- Dereham
- Diss
- Dunston Hall
- Eagles Golf Centre
- Eaton
- Fakenham
- Feltwell
- Gorleston
- Great Yarmouth & Caister
- Heacham Manor
- Hunstanton
- Kings Lynn
- Links Country Park
- Mattishall
- Middleton Hall
- Mundesley
- Norfolk Premier
- Rookery Park
- Royal Cromer
- Royal Norwich
- Royal West Norfolk
- Ryston Park
- Searles Leisure Resort
- Sheringham
- Sprowston Manor Hotel
- Swaffham
- Tydd St Giles
- Wensum Valley

North Yorkshire

- Allerthorpe
- Ampleforth College
- Bedale
- Bentham
- Catterick
- Cleveland
- Drax
- Easingwold
- Filey
- Forest of Galtres
- Forest Park
- Fulford
- Ganton
- Gilling Castle
- Harrogate
- Heworth
- Hunley Hotel
- Kirkbymoorside
- Knaresborough
- Malton & Norton
- Masham
- Middlesbrough
- Middlesbrough Municipal
- Oakdale

North Yorkshire (cont…)

- Pannal ○
- Richmond (Yorks) ○
- Romanby ○
- Saltburn-by-the-Sea ○
- Scalm Park ○
- Scarborough South Cliff ○
- Settle & Giggleswick ○
- Swallow Hall ○
- The Kp Club ○
- Thirsk & Northallerton ○
- Whitby ○
- York ○
- Pike Hills ○
- Ripon City ○
- Rudding Park Hotel Spa ○
- Sandburn Hall ○
- Scarborough North Cliff ○
- Selby ○
- Skipton ○
- Tadcaster ○
- The Oaks ○
- Wensleydale ○
- Wilton ○
- York Academy ○

Northamptonshire

- Brampton Heath ○
- Collingtree Park ○
- Delapre ○
- Kettering ○
- Northampton ○
- Overstone Park ○
- Rushden ○
- The Pytchley ○
- Whittlebury Park ○
- Cold Ashby ○
- Daventry & District ○
- Hellidon Lakes ○
- Kingsthorpe ○
- Northamptonshire County ○
- Priors Hall ○
- Staverton Park ○
- Wellingborough ○

Northumberland

- Allendale ○
- Alnmouth Village ○
- Arcot Hall ○
- Bedlingtonshire ○
- Berwick-upon-Tweed Goswick ○
- Burgham Park ○
- Haltwhistle ○
- Linden Hall ○
- Magdalene Fields ○
- Alnmouth ○
- Alnwick Castle ○
- Bamburgh Castle ○
- Bellingham ○
- Blyth ○
- Dunstanburgh Castle ○
- Hexham ○
- Longhirst Hall ○
- Newbiggin ○

Northumberland (cont…)

Prudhoe ○	Rothbury ○
Seahouses ○	Slaley Hall ○
Tynedale ○	Warkworth ○
Wooler ○	

Nottinghamshire

Beeston Fields ○	Bondhay ○
Brierley Forest ○	Bulwell Forest ○
Chilwell Manor ○	College Pines ○
Coxmoor ○	Edwalton ○
Hollinwell ○	Kilton Forest ○
Leen Valley ○	Lindrick ○
Mansfield Woodhouse ○	Mapperley ○
Newark ○	Norwood Park ○
Nottingham City ○	Notts Ladies ○
Oakmere Park ○	Radcliffe-on-Trent ○
Ramsdale Park ○	Retford ○
Ruddington Grange ○	Rufford Park ○
Sherwood Forest ○	Springwater ○
Stanton-on-the-Wolds ○	The Nottinghamshire ○
Trent Lock ○	Wollaton Park ○
Worksop ○	

Oxfordshire

Badgemore Park ○	Bicester Hotel ○
Burford ○	Cherwell Edge ○
Cotswolds Club ○	Drayton Park ○
Feldon Valley ○	Frilford Heath ○
Hadden Hill ○	Henley ○
Park Resort ○	Hinksey Heights ○
Huntercombe ○	Kirtlington ○
North Oxford ○	Oxford ○
Radley ○	Rye Hill ○
Studley Wood ○	Tadmarton Heath ○

Oxfordshire (cont…)

Thames Valley	○	The Oxfordshire	○
The Springs	○	The Wychwood	○
Waterstock	○	Witney Lakes	○

Rutland

Greetham Valley	○	Luffenham Heath	○
Rutland Water	○	Woolfox	○

Shropshire

Aqualate	○	Arscott	○
Bridgnorth	○	Chesterton Valley	○
Church Stretton	○	Hawkstone Park	○
Hill Valley	○	Horsehay Village	○
Lilleshall Hall	○	Llanymynech	○
Ludlow	○	Market Drayton	○
Meole Brace	○	Mile End	○
Oswestry	○	Shifnal	○
Shrewsbury	○	Telford	○
The Astbury	○	The Shropshire	○
Worfield	○	Wrekin	○

Somerset

Bath	○	Bleadon Hill	○
Brean	○	Burnham & Berrow	○
Cannington	○	Cricket St Thomas	○
Enmore Park	○	Fosseway	○
Henstridge	○	Isle of Wedmore	○
Kingweston	○	Lansdown	○
Mendip	○	Minehead & West Somerset	○
Oake Manor	○	Orchardleigh	○
Tall Pines	○	Taunton & Pickeridge	○
Vivary Park	○	Wells	○

Somerset (cont…)

Weston-Super-Mare	○	Wheathill	○
Wincanton	○	Worlebury	○
Yeovil	○		

South Yorkshire

Abbeydale	○	Barnsley	○
Bawtry	○	Beauchief	○
Birley Wood	○	Concord Park	○
Crookhill Park	○	Doncaster	○
Doncaster Town Moor	○	Dore & Totley	○
Grange Park	○	Hallamshire	○
Hickleton	○	Hillsborough	○
Lees Hall	○	Owston Hall	○
Phoenix	○	Renishaw Park	○
Rother Valley	○	Rotherham	○
Roundwood	○	Sandhill	○
Serlby Park	○	Silkstone	○
Sitwell Park	○	Stocksbridge	○
Styrrup Hall	○	Tankersley Park	○
Thorne	○	Thornhurst Park	○
Tinsley Park	○	Waterfront	○
Wath	○	Wheatley	○
Wombwell Hillies	○	Wortley	○

Staffordshire

Alsager	○	Barlaston	○
Beau Desert	○	Blythe Bridge	○
Branston	○	Brocton Hall	○
Burslem	○	Cannock Park	○
Darnford Moors	○	Denstone College	○
Drayton Park	○	Greenway Hall	○
Halfpenny Green	○	Ingestre Park	○
Lichfield	○	Manor	○
Newcastle-under-Lyme	○	Stafford Castle	○

Staffordshire (cont…)

- Stone O
- Trentham O
- Uttoxeter O
- Whittington Heath O
- The Chase O
- Trentham Park O
- Westwood O
- Wolstanton O

Suffolk

- Aldeburgh O
- Bramford O
- Bungay & Waveney Valley O
- Flempton O
- Halesworth O
- Hintlesham O
- Links O
- Royal Worlington & Newmarket O
- Seckford O
- St Audrys O
- Stowmarket O
- Thorpeness O
- Woodbridge O
- Beccles O
- Brett Vale O
- Bury St Edmunds O
- Fynn Valley O
- Haverhill O
- Ipswich O
- Newton Green O
- Rushmere O
- Southwold O
- St Clements O
- The Suffolk O
- Ufford Park Woodbridge O

Surrey

- Abbey Moor O
- Addington Palace O
- Beaverbrook O
- Bletchingley O
- Bramley O
- Burhill O
- Chipstead O
- Clandon O
- Coombe Hill O
- Coulsdon Court O
- Croham Hurst O
- Dorking O
- Effingham O
- Addington Court O
- Banstead Downs O
- Betchworth Park O
- Braeside O
- Bridley Artisans O
- Camberley Heath O
- Chobham O
- Clandon Regis O
- Coombe Wood O
- Cranleigh O
- Cuddington O
- Drift O
- Epsom O

Surrey (cont…)

Farleigh	O	Farnham	O
Forest Artisans	O	Foxhills	O
Gatton Manor	O	Gresham Artisan	O
Guildford	O	Hampton Court Palace	O
Hankley Common	O	Hersham	O
Hindhead	O	Hoebridge	O
Horne Park	O	Horton Park	O
Hurtmore	O	Kingswood	O
Leatherhead	O	Limpsfield Chart	O
Lingfield Park	O	Malden	O
Milford	O	New Zealand	O
North Downs	O	Oaks	O
Pachesham	O	Pine Ridge	O
Purley Downs	O	Puttenham	O
Pyrford	O	Queenwood	O
Reigate Heath	O	Reigate Hill	O
Richmond	O	Royal Automobile Club	O
Royal Mid Surrey	O	Sandown Park	O
Shirley Park	O	Silvermere	O
St Georges Hill	O	Stage	O
Surbiton	O	Surrey Downs	O
Surrey National	O	Sutton Green	O
Tandridge	O	hames Ditton & Esher	O
The Addington	O	The Wisley	O
Tyrrells Wood	O	Walton Heath	O
Wentworth Club	O	West Byfleet	O
West Hill	O	West Surrey	O
Windlemere Ladies	O	Windlesham	O
Woking	O	Woldingham	O
Woodcote Park	O	Worplesdon	O

GOLF COURSE DIRECTORY: ENGLAND

Tyne and Wear

- Abbey Moor ○
- Backworth ○
- City of Newcastle ○
- Garesfield ○
- Gosforth ○
- High Gosforth Park ○
- Houghton-Le-Spring ○
- Morpeth ○
- Ponteland ○
- Ryton ○
- Stocksfield ○
- Tynemouth ○
- Wallsend ○
- Westerhope ○
- Whitburn ○
- Addington Court ○
- Boldon ○
- Close House ○
- George Washington ○
- Heworth ○
- Hobson ○
- Matfen Hall Hotel ○
- Newcastle United ○
- Ravensworth ○
- South Shields ○
- The Northumberland ○
- Tyneside ○
- Wearside ○
- Whickham ○
- Whitley Bay ○

Warwickshire

- Ansty ○
- Atherstone ○
- Copsewood Grange ○
- Coventry Hearsall ○
- Kenilworth ○
- Marston Lakes ○
- Nuneaton ○
- Rugby ○
- Stoneleigh Deer Park ○
- Stratford Park Hotel ○
- The Warwickshire ○
- Whitefields ○
- Ardencote ○
- Bramcote Waters ○
- Coventry ○
- Hallmark the Welcombe ○
- Leamington & County ○
- North Warwickshire ○
- Oakridge ○
- Stonebridge ○
- Stratford Oaks ○
- Stratford-on-Avon ○
- Warwick ○
- Windmill Village Hotel ○

West Midlands

- Aston Wood ○
- Boldmere ○
- Cocks Moors Woods ○
- Dartmouth ○
- Bloxwich ○
- Calderfields ○
- Copt Heath ○
- Druids Heath ○

West Midlands (cont...)

- Dudley ○
- Enville ○
- Fulford Heath ○
- Greenfield ○
- Handsworth ○
- Harborne Church Farm ○
- Himley Hall ○
- Kings Norton ○
- Little Aston ○
- Moor Hall ○
- Olton ○
- Penn ○
- Pype Hayes ○
- Rose Hill ○
- Sedgley ○
- Solihull ○
- Sutton Coldfield ○
- The South Staffordshire ○
- Walsall ○
- Wergs ○
- Wishaw ○
- Edgbaston ○
- Forest of Arden Marriott ○
- Great Barr ○
- Halesowen ○
- Harborne ○
- Hatchford Brook ○
- Hollywood ○
- Ladbrook Park ○
- Maxstoke Park ○
- Moseley ○
- Oxley Park ○
- Perton Park ○
- Robin Hood ○
- Sandwell Park ○
- Shirley ○
- Stourbridge ○
- The Belfry Club ○
- Walmley ○
- Warley Woods ○
- West Midlands ○

West Sussex

- Ansty ○
- Avisford Park ○
- Chartham Park ○
- Copthorne ○
- Cowdray Park ○
- Goodwood ○
- Haywards Heath ○
- Horsham ○
- Lindfield ○
- Mannings Heath ○
- Rustington ○
- Singing Hills ○
- Tilgate Forest ○
- Worthing ○
- Ardencote ○
- Bognor Regis ○
- Chichester ○
- Cottesmore ○
- Cuckfield ○
- Ham Manor ○
- Hill Barn ○
- Ifield ○
- Littlehampton ○
- Pyecombe ○
- Selsey ○
- Slinfold ○
- West Sussex ○

West Yorkshire

- Baildon ○
- Bingley St Ives ○
- Bradford ○
- Bradley Park ○
- Calverley ○
- City of Wakefield ○
- Cleckheaton & District ○
- Crosland Heath ○
- Darrington ○
- East Bierley ○
- Elland ○
- Fulneck ○
- Gotts Park ○
- Halifax Bradley Hall ○
- Hanging Heaton ○
- Headley ○
- Hollins Hall Hotel & Country Club ○
- Howley Hall ○
- Ilkley ○
- Leeds Golf Centre ○
- Lightcliffe ○
- Low Laithes ○
- Meltham ○
- Moortown ○
- Northcliffe ○
- Oulton Hall ○
- Pontefract & District ○
- Rawdon ○
- Ryburn ○
- Scarcroft ○
- South Bradford ○
- The Alwoodley ○
- Todmorden ○
- Waterton Park ○
- Wetherby ○
- Willow Valley ○
- Woodsome Hall ○
- Ben Rhydding ○
- Bracken Ghyll ○
- Bradford Moor ○
- Branshaw ○
- Castlefields ○
- Clayton ○
- Cookridge Hall ○
- Crow Nest Park ○
- Dewsbury District ○
- East Morton ○
- Ferrybridge ○
- Garforth ○
- Halifax ○
- Halifax West End ○
- Headingley ○
- Hebden Bridge ○
- Horsforth ○
- Huddersfield ○
- Keighley ○
- Leeds Golf Club ○
- Longley Park ○
- Marsden ○
- Moor Allerton ○
- Normanton ○
- Otley ○
- Outlane ○
- Queensbury ○
- Roundhay Park ○
- Sand Moor ○
- Shipley ○
- Temple Newsam ○
- The Manor ○
- Wakefield ○
- West Bradford ○
- Whitwood ○
- Woodhall Hills ○
- Woolley Park ○

Wiltshire

Basset Down ○	Bowood Hotel ○
Brinkworth ○	Broome Manor ○
Chippenham ○	Cumberwell Park ○
Erlestoke ○	Hamptworth ○
High Post ○	Kingsdown ○
Marlborough ○	North Wilts ○
Oaksey Park ○	Ogbourne Downs ○
Rushmore ○	Salisbury & South Wilts ○
Shrivenham Park ○	The Defence Academy ○
The Manor House ○	The Wiltshire Hotel ○
Tidworth Garrison ○	Upavon ○
West Wilts ○	Westbury ○
Whitley ○	Wrag Barn ○

Worcestershire

Bewdley Pines ○	Blackwell ○
Bransford ○	Broadway ○
Bromsgrove ○	Churchill & Blakedown ○
Cleobury Mortimer ○	Droitwich ○
Evesham ○	Gaudet Luce ○
Grove ○	Hagley ○
Leominster ○	Little Lakes ○
Ombersley ○	Redditch ○
Ravenmeadow & Perdiswell Park ○	Redditch Kingfisher ○
Sapey ○	The Abbey Hotel ○
The Kidderminster ○	The Worcestershire ○
Vale ○	Wharton Park ○
Worcester ○	

IRELAND
TICK THE COURSES YOU'VE PLAYED...

GOLF COURSE DIRECTORY: IRELAND

Co. Carlow

Borris	○	Carlow	○
Mount Wolseley	○		

Co. Cavan

Belturbet	○	Blacklion	○
County Cavan	○	Crover House	○
Farnham Estate	○	Slieve Russell	○
Virginia	○		

Co. Clare

Clonlara	○	Doonbeg	○
Dromoland Castle	○	East Clare	○
Ennis	○	Kilkee	○
Kilrush	○	Lahinch	○
Shannon	○	Spanish Point	○
Woodstock	○		

Co. Cork

Bandon	○	Bantry Bay	○
Berehaven	○	Blarney	○
Castlemartyr	○	Chareleville	○
Clonakilty	○	Cobh	○
Cork	○	Doneraile	○
Douglas	○	East Cork	○
Fermoy	○	Fota Island	○
Glengarriff	○	Harbour Point	○
Kanturk	○	Kinsale	○
Lee Valley	○	Macroom	○
Mahon	○	Mallow	○
Mitchelstown	○	Monkstown	○
Muskerry	○	Raffeen Creek	○
Skibbereen & West Carbery	○	Youghal	○

GOLF COURSE DIRECTORY: IRELAND

Co. Donegal

Ballybofey & Stranorlar	○	Ballyliffin	○
Buncrana	○	Bundoran	○
Cloughaneely	○	Cruit Island	○
Donegal	○	Dunfanaghy	○
Greencastle	○	Gweedore	○
Letterkenny	○	Narin & Portnoo	○
North West	○	Otway	○
Portsalon	○	Redcastle	○
Rosapenna	○		

Co. Dublin

Balbriggan	○	Balcarrick	○
Ballinascorney	○	Beaverstown	○
Beech Park	○	Butter Mountain	○
Carrickmines	○	Castle	○
Castleknock	○	Clontarf	○
Corballis Links	○	Corrstown	○
Deer Park	○	Donabate	○
Dun Laoghaire	○	Edmondstown	○
Elm Park	○	Elmgreen	○
Forrest Little	○	Foxrock	○
Grange	○	Grange Castle	○
Hermitage	○	Hollywood Lakes	○
Howth	○	Killiney	○
Jameson Links Portmarnock	○	Kilmashogue	○
Leopardstown	○	Lisheen Springs	○
Lucan	○	Luttrellstown Castle	○
Malahide	○	Milltown	○
Newlands	○	Portmarnock	○
Rathfarnham	○	Roganstown	○
Royal Dublin	○	Rush	○
Silloge Park	○	Skerries	○
Slade Valley	○	St Anne's	○
St Margarets	○	Stackstown	○
Sutton	○	Swords	○
The Island	○	Westmanstown	○

GOLF COURSE DIRECTORY: IRELAND

Co. Galway

Athenry	○	Ballinasloe	○
Bearna	○	Connemara	○
Connemara Isles	○	Cregmore Park	○
Dunmore Demesne	○	Galway	○
Galway Bay	○	Glenlo Abbey	○
Gort	○	Loughrea	○
Mountbellew	○	Oughterard	○
Portumna	○	Tuam	○

Co. Kerry

Ballybunion	○	Ballyheigue Castle	○
Beaufort	○	Castlegregory	○
Castleisland	○	Castlerosse	○
Ceann Sibeal	○	Dooks	○
Kenmare	○	Killarney	○
Maine Valley	○	Parknasilla	○
Ring of Kerry	○	Ross	○
Tralee	○	Waterville	○

Co. Kildare

Athy	○	Carton House	○
Castlewarden	○	Celbridge Elm Hall	○
Cill Dara	○	Clane	○
Craddockstown	○	Edenderry	○
Hibernian	○	Highfield	○
Kilkea Castle	○	Killeen	○
Millicent	○	Moyvalley	○
Naas	○	Newbridge	○
Palmerstown House Estate	○	Royal Curragh	○
Straffan	○	The K Club	○

Co. Kilkenny

- Callan ○
- Gowran Park ○
- Mount Juliet ○
- Castlecomer ○
- Kilkenny ○

Co. Laois

- Abbeyleix ○
- Portarlington ○
- Rathdowney ○
- The Heritage ○
- Mountrath ○
- Portlaoise ○
- The Heath ○

Co. Leitrim

- Ballinamore ○

Co. Limerick

- Adare ○
- Ballyneety ○
- Limerick ○
- Rathbane ○
- Adare Manor ○
- Castletroy ○
- Newcastle West ○

Co. Longford

- County Longford ○

Co. Louth

- Ardee ○
- Dundalk ○
- Seapoint ○
- County Louth ○
- Greenore ○

GOLF COURSE DIRECTORY: IRELAND

Co. Mayo

Achill Island	○	Ballina	○
Ballinrobe	○	Ballyhaunis	○
Belmullet	○	Castlebar	○
Claremorris	○	Mulranny	○
Swinford	○	Westport	○

Co. Meath

Ashbourne	○	Bellewstown	○
Black Bush	○	County Meath	○
Headfort	○	Kilcock	○
Killeen Castle	○	Knightsbrook	○
Laytown & Bettystown	○	Rathcore	○
Royal Tara	○	South Meath	○
Summerhill	○		

Co. Monaghan

Clones	○	Concra Wood Castleblayney	○
Mannan Castle	○	Nuremore	○
Rossmore	○		

Co. Offaly

Birr	○	Esker Hills	○
Tullamore	○		

Co. Roscommon

Athlone	○	Ballaghaderreen	○
Boyle	○	Carrick-on-Shannon	○
Castlerea	○	Roscommon	○
Strokestown	○		

GOLF COURSE DIRECTORY: IRELAND

Co. Sligo

- Castle Dargan ○
- County Sligo ○
- Enniscrone ○
- Strandhill ○
- Tubbercurry ○

Co. Tipperary

- Ballykisteen ○
- Cahir Park ○
- Clonmel ○
- County Tipperary ○
- Nenagh ○
- Roscrea ○
- Slievenamon ○
- Templemore ○
- Thurles ○
- Tipperary ○

Co. Waterford

- Carrick-on-Suir ○
- Dungarvan ○
- Dunmore East ○
- Faithlegg ○
- Gold Coast ○
- Lismore ○
- Tramore ○
- Waterford ○
- Waterford Castle ○
- West Waterford ○
- Williamstown ○

Co. Westmeath

- Glasson ○
- Moate ○
- Mount Temple ○
- Mullingar ○
- New Forest ○

Co. Wexford

- Ballymoney ○
- Bunclody ○
- Courtown ○
- Enniscorthy ○
- New Ross ○
- Rosslare ○
- St Helen's Bay ○
- Tara Glen ○
- Wexford ○

Co. Wicklow

Arklow	O	Baltinglass	O
Blainroe	O	Blessington Lakes	O
Bray	O	Coollatin	O
Delgany	O	Druids Glen	O
Druid's Heath	O	European Club	O
Greystones	O	Macreddin	O
Old Conna	O	Powerscourt	O
Rathsallagh	O	Roundwood	O
Tulfarris	O	Wicklow	O
Woodbrook	O	Woodenbridge	O

NORTHERN
IRELAND
TICK THE COURSES YOU'VE PLAYED...

GOLF COURSE DIRECTORY: NORTHERN IRELAND

Co. Antrim

Aberdelghy	○	Antrim	○
Ballycastle	○	Ballyclare	○
Ballymena	○	Balmoral	○
Belvoir Park	○	Bushfoot	○
Cairndhu	○	Carrickfergus	○
Castlereagh Hills	○	City of Belfast	○
Cliftonville	○	Colin Valley	○
Cushendall	○	Down Royal	○
Dunmurry	○	Fortwilliam	○
Galgorm Castle	○	Gracehill	○
Greenacres	○	Greenisland	○
Hilton Templepatrick	○	Lambeg	○
Larne	○	Lisburn	○
Malone	○	Massereene	○
Ormeau	○	Rathmore	○
Rockmount	○	Royal Portrush	○
Shandon Park	○	Temple	○
Whitehead	○		

Co. Armagh

Cloverhill	○	County Armagh	○
Edenmore	○	Loughgall	○
Lurgan	○	Portadown	○
Silverwood	○	Tandragee	○

Co. Down

Ardglass	○	Ardminnan	○
Ashfield	○	Banbridge	○
Bangor	○	Blackwood Mahee	○
Bright Castle	○	Carnalea	○
Clandeboye	○	Crossgar	○
Donaghadee	○	Helen's Bay	○
Holywood	○	Kilkeel	○
Kirkistown Castle	○	Knock	○

Co. Down (cont…)

Mayobridge	O	Mourne	O
Royal Belfast	O	Royal County Down	O
Scrabo	O	Spa	O
St Patrick's	O	Warrenpoint	O

Co. Fermanagh

Castle Hume	O	Enniskillen	O
Lough Erne	O		

Co. Londonderry

Castlerock	O	City of Derry	O
Faughan Valley	O	Foyle	O
Kilrea	O	Manor	O
Moyola Park	O	Portstewart	O
Roe Park	O		

Co. Tyrone

Aughnacloy	O	Clogher Valley	O
Dungannon	O	Fintona	O
Killymoon	O	Newtownstewart	O
Omagh	O	Strabane	O

SCOTLAND
TICK THE COURSES YOU'VE PLAYED...

GOLF COURSE DIRECTORY: SCOTLAND

Aberdeen City

- Aberdeen Ladies ○
- Auchmill ○
- Caledonian ○
- Deeside ○
- Murcar Links ○
- Northern ○
- Royal Aberdeen ○
- Aberdeen Petroleum ○
- Bon Accord ○
- Craibstone ○
- Hazlehead ○
- Nigg Bay ○
- Peterculter ○

Aberdeenshire

- Aboyne ○
- Auchenblae ○
- Ballindalloch Castle ○
- Banchory ○
- Cruden Bay ○
- Dufftown ○
- Fraserburgh ○
- Inchmarlo ○
- Inverallochy ○
- Kemnay ○
- Longside ○
- McDonald ○
- Newburg-on-Ythan ○
- Oldmeldrum ○
- Peterhead ○
- Rosehearty ○
- Stonehaven ○
- Torphins ○
- Turriff ○
- Alford ○
- Ballater ○
- Balmoral Castle ○
- Braemar ○
- Duff House Royal ○
- Dunecht House ○
- Huntly ○
- Insch ○
- Inverurie ○
- Kintore ○
- Lumphanan ○
- Meldrum House ○
- Newmachar ○
- Paul Lawrie ○
- Portlethen ○
- Royal Tarlair ○
- Tarland ○
- Trump International ○
- Westhill ○

GOLF COURSE DIRECTORY: SCOTLAND

Angus

- Arbroath Artisan ○
- Carnoustie ○
- Carnoustie Links ○
- Dalhousie ○
- Forfar ○
- Kirriemuir ○
- Letham Grange ○
- Montrose Caledonia ○
- Panmure ○
- Royal Montrose Mercantile ○
- Brechin ○
- Carnoustie Caledonia ○
- Carnoustie Mercantile ○
- Edzell ○
- Grange & Broughty ○
- Ladies Panmure Monifieth ○
- Monifieth ○
- Montrose Links ○
- Piperdam ○
- Station Master ○

Argyll & Bute

- Ardfin Estate ○
- Blairmore & Strone ○
- Carradale ○
- Craignure ○
- Dragon's Tooth ○
- Dunoon ○
- Helensburgh ○
- Inveraray ○
- Isle of Seil ○
- Lochgilphead ○
- Machrihanish Dunes ○
- Rothesay ○
- Taynuilt ○
- Tobermory ○
- Woodlands Glencoe ○
- Ballachulish ○
- Bute ○
- Cowal ○
- Dalmally ○
- Dunaverty ○
- Glencruitten ○
- Innellan ○
- Islay ○
- Kyles of Bute ○
- Lochgoilhead ○
- Port Bannatyne ○
- Tarbert ○
- The Machrihanish ○
- Vaul ○

GOLF COURSE DIRECTORY: SCOTLAND

City of Edinburgh

- Baberton ○
- Braids United ○
- Carrick Knowe ○
- Craigentinny ○
- Duddingston ○
- Edinburgh Thistle ○
- Gogarburn ○
- Kingsknowe ○
- Merchants of Edinburgh ○
- Murrayfield ○
- Prestonfield ○
- Royal Burgess Society of Edinburgh ○
- Silverknowes ○
- Turnhouse ○
- Braid Hills ○
- Bruntsfield Links ○
- Carrickvale ○
- Craigmillar ○
- Dundas Parks ○
- Edinburgh Western ○
- Harrison ○
- Lochend ○
- Mortonhall ○
- Portobello ○
- Ratho Park ○
- Ravelston ○
- Swanston ○
- Wee Braids ○

Clackmannanshire

- Alloa ○
- Braehead (Alloa) ○
- Tillicoultry ○
- Alva ○
- Muckhart ○

Dumfries & Galloway

- Brighouse Bay ○
- Colvend ○
- Dalbeattie ○
- Dumfries & Galloway ○
- Kirkcudbright ○
- Lochmaben ○
- Moffat ○
- Newton Stewart ○
- Powfoot ○
- Southerness ○
- Stranraer ○
- Wigtown & Bladnoch ○
- Castle Douglas ○
- Crichton ○
- Dumfries & County ○
- Gatehouse ○
- Langholm ○
- Lockerbie ○
- New Galloway ○
- Portpatrick Dunskey ○
- Sanquhar ○
- St Medan ○
- Thornhill ○
- Wigtownshire County ○

Dundee City

Ballumbie Castle ○ Caird Park ○
Downfield ○ Kettledrum ○
Kingennie ○ Logie ○

East Ayrshire

Annanhill ○ Ballochmyle ○
Caprington ○ Crosshouse ○
Doon Valley ○ Loudoun ○
Muirkirk ○ New Cumnock ○
Portmann ○ Rowallan Castle ○
Stewarton ○

East Dunbartonshire

Balmore ○ Bearsden ○
Bishopbriggs ○ Campsie ○
Cawder ○ Clober ○
Dougalston ○ Douglas Park ○
Hayston ○ Hilton Park ○
Kirkintilloch ○ Lenzie ○
Littlehill ○ Milngavie ○
Windyhill ○

East Lothian

Archerfield Links ○ Bass Rock ○
Castle Park ○ Craigielaw ○
Dunbar ○ Gifford ○
Glen ○ Gullane ○
Haddington ○ Longniddry ○
Luffness New ○ Marine ○
Musselburgh ○ Musselburgh Old Course ○
North Berwick ○ Renaissance ○
Rhodes ○ Royal Musselburgh ○
Tantallon ○ Winterfield ○

GOLF COURSE DIRECTORY: SCOTLAND

East Renfrewshire

Bonnyton	○	Caldwell	○
Cathcart Castle	○	East Renfrewshire	○
Fereneze	○	Mearns Castle	○
Shaws Bar	○	Wallacetown	○
Whitecraigs	○	Williamwood	○

Eilean Siar (Western Isles)

Askernish	○	Benbecula	○
Isle of Barra	○	Isle of Harris	○
Stornoway	○		

Falkirk

Bonnybridge	○	Braes	○
Falkirk	○	Falkirk Tryst	○
Glenbervie	○	Grangemouth	○

Fife

Aberdour	○	Anstruther	○
Auchterderran	○	Balbirnie Park	○
Burntisland	○	Canmore	○
Charleton	○	Cluny	○
Cowdenbeath	○	Crail	○
Cupar	○	Drumoig	○
Dukes, St Andrews	○	Dumbarnie	○
Dunfermline	○	Dunnikier Park	○
Earlsferry Thistle	○	Eden Club	○
Edenfields	○	Elie & Earlsferry Ladies	○
Elie Sports Club	○	Elmwood Society	○
Fairmont St Andrews	○	Falkland	○
Forrester Park	○	Glenrothes	○
Golf House Club Elie	○	Kinghorn	○
Kingsbarns	○	Kirkcaldy	○
Ladybank	○	Leslie	○

Fife (cont…)

- Leuchars Station ○
- Leven Thistle ○
- Lochore Meadows ○
- MGR ○
- Pitreavie (Dunfermline) ○
- Saline ○
- Scoonie ○
- St Andrews ○
- St Andrews Thistle ○
- St Michaels ○
- St Rule Club ○
- Tulliallan ○
- Leven ○
- Lochgelly ○
- Lundin ○
- New GC St Andrews ○
- Royal & Ancient St Andrews ○
- SALJGA ○
- Scotscraig ○
- St Andrews Links Trust ○
- StLeonards ○
- St Regulus Ladies ○
- Thornton ○
- University of St Andrews ○

Glasgow City

- Cowglen ○
- Deaconsbank ○
- Golf It! ○
- Knightswood ○
- Sandyhills ○
- David Lloyd Rouken Glen ○
- Glasgow Victoria ○
- Haggs Castle ○
- Pollok ○

Highland

- Abernethy ○
- Alness ○
- Bonar Bridge & Ardgay ○
- Carnegie Club at Skibo Castle ○
- Castle Stuart ○
- Eriskay Whisky Galore ○
- Fort William ○
- Gairloch ○
- Grantown-on-Spey ○
- Invergordon ○
- Isle of Skye ○
- Kingussie ○
- Lybster ○
- Aigas ○
- Boat of Garten ○
- Brora ○
- Carrbridge ○
- Durness ○
- Fort Augustus ○
- Fortrose & Rosemarkie ○
- Golspie ○
- Helmsdale ○
- Inverness ○
- Kings ○
- Lochcarron ○
- Muir of Ord ○

GOLF COURSE DIRECTORY: SCOTLAND

Highland (cont...)

- Nairn
- Newtonmore
- Reay
- Spean Bridge
- Strathpeffer Spa
- Thurso
- Ullapool
- Nairn Dunbar
- Portmahomack
- Royal Dornoch
- Spey Valley
- Tain
- Traigh
- Wick

Inverclyde

- Gourock
- Greenock Whinhill
- Greenock
- Port Glasgow

Midlothian

- Broomieknowe
- Kings Acre
- Melville
- Whitehill House
- Glencorse
- Liberton
- Newbattle

Moray

- Buckpool
- Elgin
- Garmouth & Kingston
- Keith
- Moray
- Spey Bay
- Cullen Links
- Forres
- Hopeman
- Maverston
- Rothes
- Strathlene Buckie

GOLF COURSE DIRECTORY: SCOTLAND

North Ayrshire

Ardeer	O	Auchenharvie	O
Beith	O	Brodick	O
Corrie	O	Irvine Ravenspark	O
Kidsneuk Ladies	O	Kilbirnie Place	O
Lamlash	O	Largs	O
Machrie Bay	O	Millport	O
Moorpark	O	Routenburn	O
Shiskine	O	Skelmorlie	O
The Irvine	O	West Kilbride	O
Western Gailes	O	Whiting Bay	O

North Lanarkshire

Airdrie	O	Bellshill	O
Colville Park	O	Crow Wood	O
Dalziel Park	O	Drumpellier	O
Dullatur	O	Easter Moffat	O
Kilsyth Lennox	O	Lisini 9	O
Lochview	O	Palacerigg	O
Shotts	O	Torrance Park	O
Westerwood	O	Wishaw	O

Orkney Islands

Orkney	O	South Ronaldsay	O
Stromnes	O		

GOLF COURSE DIRECTORY: SCOTLAND

Perth & Kinross

- Aberfeldy ○
- Auchterarder ○
- Blair Atholl ○
- Comrie ○
- Crieff ○
- Dun Ochil ○
- Dunkeld & Birnam ○
- Gleneagles ○
- Kenmore/Mains of Taymouth ○
- King James VI ○
- Milnathort ○
- Muthill ○
- Perth Artisans ○
- Pitlochry ○
- Strathmore ○
- Taymouth Castle ○
- Alyth ○
- Bishopshire ○
- Blairgowrie ○
- Craigie Hall ○
- Dalmunzie ○
- Dun Whinny ○
- Dunning ○
- Glenearn ○
- Kilspindie ○
- Kinross ○
- Murrayshall ○
- North Inch Junior ○
- Perth Railway ○
- St Fillans ○
- Strathtay ○
- Whitemuir ○

Renfrewshire

- Barshaw ○
- Earl of Mar ○
- Erskine ○
- Kilmacolm ○
- Malletsheugh ○
- Paisley ○
- Ranfurly Castle ○
- Cochrane Castle ○
- Elderslie ○
- Gleddoch Resorts ○
- Lochwinnoch ○
- Old Course Ranfurly ○
- Ralston ○
- Renfrew ○

GOLF COURSE DIRECTORY: SCOTLAND

Scottish Borders

Cardrona	○	Duns	○
Eyemouth	○	Galashiels	○
Hawick	○	Hirsel	○
Innerleithen	○	Jedburgh	○
Kelso	○	Lauder	○
Lilliardsedge	○	Melrose	○
Minto	○	Newcastleton	○
Peebles	○	Roxburghe Hotel	○
Selkirk	○	St Boswells	○
Torwoodlee	○	West Linton	○
Woll	○		

South Ayrshire

Abbotsford	○	Ayr Carrick	○
Ayr Seafield	○	Belleisle Park	○
Carrick Speakers	○	Chase	○
Dalmilling Parkland	○	Drongan	○
Dundonald Links	○	Fullarton	○
Girvan	○	Golf South Ayrshire	○
Kilmarnock (Barassie)	○	Ladies Troon	○
Maybole	○	NB Parkstone	○
Pontoon	○	Prestwick	○
Prestwick St Cuthbert	○	Prestwick St Nicholas	○
Royal Troon	○	Troon Bentinck Ladies	○
Troon Merchants	○	Troon Portland	○
Troon St Meddans	○	Troon Welbeck	○
Trump Turnberry	○	Turnberry	○

South Lanarkshire

Ayr Neptune	○	Biggar	○
Bothwell Castle	○	Calderbraes	○
Cambuslang	○	Carluke	○
Carnwath	○	Cathkin Braes	○
Douglas Water	○	East Kilbride	○

GOLF COURSE DIRECTORY: SCOTLAND

South Lanarkshire (cont…)

- East Kilbride Sports Club ○
- Hamilton ○
- Kirkhill ○
- Langlands ○
- Leadhills ○
- Ross Priory ○
- Strathclyde Park ○
- Greenhills ○
- Hollandbush ○
- Lanark ○
- Larkhall ○
- Playsport ○
- Strathaven ○
- Torrance House ○

Stirling

- Aberfoyle ○
- Bridge of Allan ○
- Callander ○
- Killin ○
- Strathendric ○
- Balfron ○
- Buchanan Castle ○
- Dunblane New ○
- Stirling ○

West Dunbartonshire

- Cardross ○
- Clydebank & District ○
- Clydeview & Cleddans ○
- Dumbarton ○
- Radnor Park ○
- Carrick at Cameron House ○
- Clydebank Overtoun ○
- Dalmuir ○
- Loch Lomond ○
- Vale of Leven ○

West Lothian

- Bathgate ○
- Bridgend & District ○
- Deer Park ○
- Harburn ○
- Linlithgow ○
- Polkemmet ○
- Uphall ○
- Binny ○
- Dalmahoy Hotel ○
- Greenburn ○
- Kingsfield ○
- Niddry Castle ○
- Pumpherston ○
- West Lothian ○

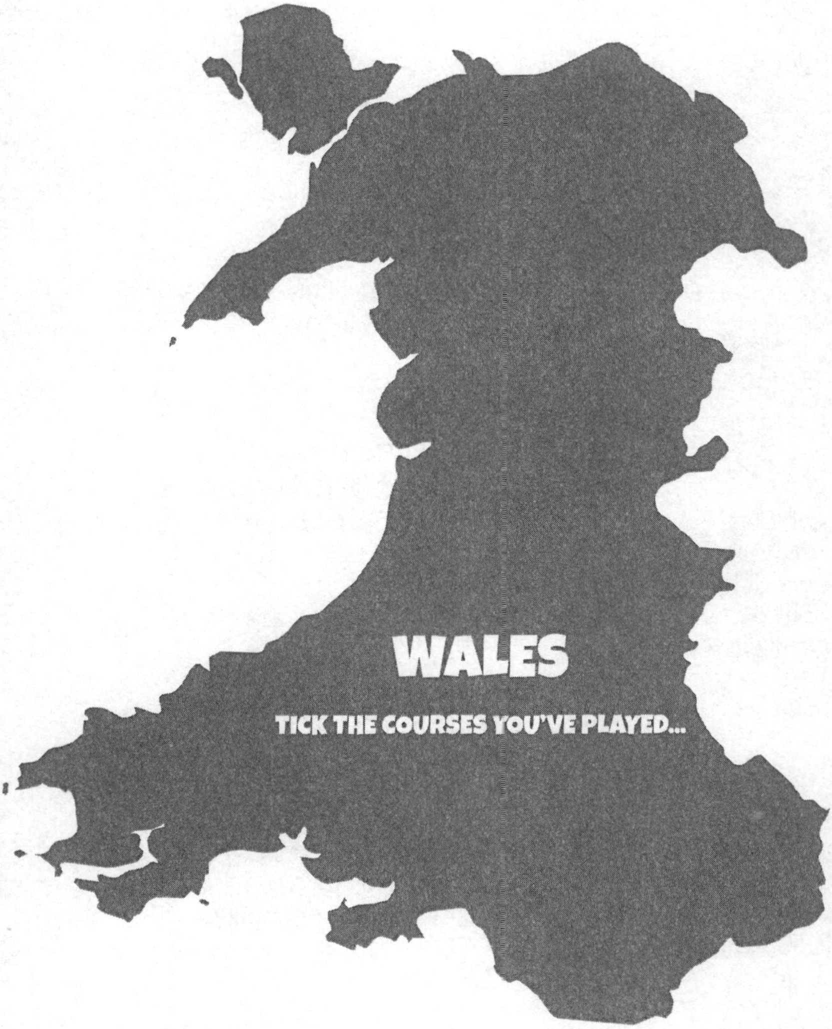

WALES

TICK THE COURSES YOU'VE PLAYED...

GOLF COURSE DIRECTORY: WALES

Blaenau Gwent

- Parc Bryn Bach ○
- Tredegar & Rhymney ○

Bridgend

- Bridgend ○
- Grove ○
- Coed-Y-Mwstwr ○
- Pyle & Kenfig ○

Caerphilly

- Brynmeadows Hotel & Spa ○
- Ridgeway ○
- Caerphilly ○
- Whitehall ○

Cardiff

- Cardiff ○
- Castell Coch ○
- Cottrell Park ○
- Peterstone Lakes ○
- St Mellons ○
- Whitchurch (Cardiff) ○
- Cardiff Golf Centre ○
- Castle Heights ○
- Creigiau ○
- Radyr ○
- Wenvoe Castle ○

Carmarthenshire

- Ashburnham ○
- Derllys Court ○
- Glyn Abbey ○
- Llandovery College ○
- Pembrey Country Park ○
- Werndd ○
- Carmarthen ○
- Garnant Park ○
- Glynhir ○
- Machynys Peninsula ○
- Tycroes ○

GOLF COURSE DIRECTORY: WALES

Ceredigion

Aberystwyth	○	Borth & Ynyslas	○
Cardigan	○	Cilgwyn	○
Cliff Hotel	○	Cwmrhydneuadd	○
Penrhos Park	○		

Conwy

Abergele	○	Betws Y Coed	○
Conwy	○	Great Orme	○
Llanfairfehan	○	Maesdu	○
North Wales	○	Old Colwyn	○
Penmaenmawr	○	Rhos-on-Sea	○

Denbighshire

Denbigh	○	Kinmel Park	○
Prestatyn	○	Rhuddlan	○
Rhyl	○	Ruthin Pwllglas	○
St Melyd	○	Vale Golf Centre	○
Vale of Llangollen	○		

Flintshire

Flint	○	Flint Mountain Park	○
Hawarden	○	Holywell	○
Mold	○	Old Padeswood	○
Padeswood & Buckley	○	Pennant Park	○

GOLF COURSE DIRECTORY: WALES

Gwynedd

Aberdovey	○	Abersoch	○
Bala	○	Baron Hill	○
Bull Bay	○	Caernarfon	○
Fairbourne	○	Llyn	○
Nefyn & District	○	Porthmadog	○
Pwllheli	○	Royal St David's	○
St Deiniol	○	Storws Wen	○
Tyddyn Mawr	○		

Isle of Anglesey

Anglesey	○	Henllys	○
Holyhead	○	Llangefni	○

Merthyr Tydfil

Morlais Castle	○

Monmouthshire

Llanishen	○	Marriott St Pierre	○
Monmouth	○	Monmouthshire	○
The Rolls of Monmouth	○	West Monmouthshire	○
Woodlake Park & Country Club	○		

Neath Port Talbot

Gnoll	○	Lakeside	○
Tata Stee	○		

Newport

Caerleon	○	Celtic Manor Resort	○
Llanwern	○	Newport	○
Parc	○	Tredegar Park	○

GOLF COURSE DIRECTORY: WALES

Torfaen

Blackwood O
Llanyrafon O
Pontypool O
Greenmeadow O
Pontnewydd O

Vale of Glamorgan

Aberdare O
Bargoed O
Celtic Minor O
Fairwood Park O
Glynneath O
Neath O
Southerndown O
St Athan O
The Vale Resort O
Aberdulais O
Brynhill O
Dinas Powis O
Glamorganshire O
Hensol O
Royal Porthcawl O
St Andrews Major O
Swansea Bay O

Wrexham

Clays O
Plassey O
Moss Valley O
Wrexham O

* 9 7 8 1 8 0 4 6 7 8 0 9 1 *

BV - #0107 - 030624 - C0 - 216/138/10 - PB - 9781804678091 - Gloss Lamination